The Manual

Understanding
Your
Congregation
As A System

GEORGE PARSONS & SPEED B. LEAS

An Alban Institute Publication

The Publications Program of The Alban Institute is assisted by a grant from Trinity Church, New York.

Library of Congress Catalog Card Number 93-73158
ISBN 1-56699-118-8

CONTENTS

PREFACE

A noted family therapist once commented that she had grown tired of pulling families out of the river. Instead, she decided to walk upstream to see why they were falling in. In this spirit, two conflict management consultants, with a combined thirty-three years of experience working with severely conflicted congregations, here turn our attention to the sources of organizational health and vitality in the church.

We are not interested in "conflict prevention." We know that a vital congregation can usually turn its face toward conflict and work with its differences. We are interested in creating organizational vitality—in helping congregations develop healthy, effective organizations within which ministry can flourish.

When congregations exhibit strong program life, vibrant fellowship, effective outreach to their community, or meaningful worship, they do so because they have given adequate attention to the vessel that carries all of these elements. The content of ministry is powerfully determined by the organizational system, by the vessel that surrounds it. The Congregational Systems Inventory (CSI) is based on learnings from systems theory and organizational architecture. It will help you look carefully at the vessel and at the processes through which you create ministry and the systems that sustain your efforts.

The CSI is an evaluative tool to be used by congregational leaders as they prepare for or respond to changes in the lives of their congregations. It is particularly useful when congregations are

— coping with numerical growth
— coping with numerical decline
— anticipating a building or capital campaign

— moving through a pastoral transition
— preparing for long-range planning
— anticipating staff changes
— facing a significant change in the demographics of the
  surrounding community
— recovering from an organizational trauma

The inventory is best used with the staff, members of the main church board, and other key lay leaders. To assess your congregation's organizational life, we suggest you ask staff, board members, and key lay leaders to complete the inventory individually; then compile the composite score of these leaders. By so doing, you take advantage of the variety of perspectives present within the leadership. Your large sample of viewpoints captures the complexities of the congregation's life.

This manual is a companion to the Congregational Systems Inventory Participant's Packet and is designed to help you introduce the CSI to a group of congregational leaders, to interpret the results of the inventory particularly in a composite profile, and to assess the implications of the results for a particular congregation. (Instructions for ordering copies of the CSI Participant's Packet can be found at the end of the manual.)

The authors developed this manual through a combination of collaborative and parallel effort. George Parsons wrote chapters I, III, V, and the Appendix. Speed Leas wrote chapters II and VI through XII. Chapter IV was prepared by both authors.

ACKNOWLEDGMENTS

We wish to thank Richard T. Pascale for his support and encouragement as we developed this material. Dr. Pascale provided the conceptual framework for the Congregational Systems Inventory and granted permission to incorporate his ideas into the accompanying text. We are grateful for his continued leadership in the field of organizational change and for his concern for the health of congregations.

We also thank Pat Weber Parsons, who from the very beginning of this project acted as editor, sounding board, and advocate. We are grateful to Susan Lapp for providing the integrative typing and formating that combined our separate writings. And we also wish to thank Celia Hahn for her ongoing support, her editorial help, and especially for her patient shepherding of this manuscript.

CHAPTER I

Congregational Systems Inventory Introduction: The Tyranny of Successful Habits

The seeds of decline are found in our successes. This axiom applies to people as well as to organizations. We pay a price to discover what will work in our lives. When we place ourselves (or are placed) outside of our zone of comfort, we learn and grow. Learning is usually accompanied by initial discomfort. Recall learning to ride a bike or to speak in front of a group or to deal with an angry friend. In this regard, we are all by temperament pioneers, curious about life and the world set before us, eager to find a way that works.

Yet as our pioneering produces success, we tend to become homesteaders. Our successes become our precious habits. The newly won ground becomes our home. In childhood we may have successfully learned to handle combative parents by being the appeaser, the rescuer, the problem solver, or the fighter; we embrace that success and as adults rely on that approach to conflict. Even as the time-worn approach affords fewer rewards, we are tempted to refine and depend on those habits. This is the tyranny of successful habits. As stress increases, we dependently revert to those habits, shunning experimentation. Our learned strengths eventually become our excesses.

Many congregations are stuck in their successes. They can point to an earlier time of vitality and growth and to subsequent efforts to build on their success. They can often identify their strengths and the connection between those strengths and past success. But their successes led them to embrace organizational patterns and habits that no longer serve them well. They continue to exercise the same set of muscles while the rest of the body atrophies.

Congregations "succeed" because they are able to connect their unique resources and competencies with the current needs of those inside the congregation and beyond. This organizational responsiveness (the pioneering dimension) helps congregations adapt to a changing environment and renew themselves. Most of the congregational decline we observe is the result of a church finding a pattern that worked and staying with that pattern long past its usefulness.

A vivid example is a large congregation that experienced growth and vitality in the late 1960s and early 1970s. Those successes were based on a well-planned and diversified Sunday morning adult education program, an eclectic social ministry, and a traditional Presbyterian worship experience with a few modern touches thrown in. These three strengths have continued to be the centerpiece for this congregation over the years and the congregational leaders have worked diligently to produce continuous improvement in these areas.

But gradually the population of people drawn to the church and the demographics of the neighborhood changed. The traditional kinds of members moved to outer suburbs. Housing around the church deteriorated. Dissatisfied parishioners engaged in periodic factional disputes often focused on pastoral leadership. All of these changes brought more stress, which in turn drove the congregation's habits even deeper. Adult education continues to be well planned, social ministry opportunities are plentiful, traditional worship skills have been refined—and the congregation has been in a numerical decline for fifteen years. The seeds of decline are found in a congregation's successes.

The analysis put forth by Loren Mead in his book *The Once and Future Church* provides a larger framework within which to view the tyranny of our successes. Pointing to a profound shift away from the Christendom Paradigm (in which being a citizen meant being a church member) and toward a new reality that is shaking the church at its foundation, Mead believes the church will have to reinvent itself. New directions and models will be necessary to respond to these sweeping changes. Mead writes, "It is as if the magnetic north pole moved from Greenland to Alaska, and our compasses keep flickering between the remembered pole and the new pole. In such a world it is hard to keep one's bearings."[1] Against this degree of change, individual congregations may be all the more tempted to draw even better maps to get to the remembered pole.

Current literature on organizational behavior addresses what is called the problem of organizational learning disabilities.[2] Congregational leaders are vulnerable to these learning disabilities, which include our tendency to maximize our habits: If we simply develop our strengths, we will be effective in our ministry. Inherent in this disability is our failure to see the impact of long-term events, of gradual shifts in the environment surrounding the church, or changes within the congregation itself. With this disability we also focus on the practicalities of leadership and what we must do to keep our part of the show going. As leaders we develop tunnel vision, born of the necessity of the tasks, and fail to see a holistic systemic view of the congregation. Then our definitions of the "problems" and "solutions" in congregational leadership are partial and do not take into account the interrelationship of the dimensions of a congregational system. Effective congregational leadership will demand this broader perspective. Anything less will drive us further into the tyranny of success.

We hope that the insights derived from the Congregational Systems Inventory will provide leaders with this needed glimpse into the organizational life of a congregation. The CSI is intended to help leaders step back and look at a larger picture; it points to opportunities for creative release from old habits so that a congregation can reclaim its explorer identity and develop the inner resiliency to respond to changing times and new challenges.

G. P.

CHAPTER II

Congregations as Systems

Systems Theory Axioms

Approaches to Organizational Problems

There are at least three ways to look at what is going on in organizations. Some analysts pay close attention to what individual members do, some to the problems the organization needs to solve, others to how the system is functioning. Let's look at these three approaches.

Difficult-People Approach. Recently several books have been published about antagonists or difficult people in congregations. Some of these books focus on the leaders, some on members, some on both; these authors understand organizational problems as caused by what people do or don't do.

We have no doubt that what individual people do can be problematic. A person can get a "bee in his bonnet" and become an absolute nuisance to others; he can be angry or upset—or simply unskilled—and bring his "attitude" or incompetence into the church causing havoc or slowing progress.

Recently one of us was working in an organization where the "boss," in this case a denominational executive, was unable to control his temper. When someone challenged him, he would often flare up and threaten or filibuster the person he perceived to be an enemy.

A systems approach to this problem would assume that something in the patterns and relationships of the organization itself was creating or abetting this behavior.

In this case, in our opinion, much of the difficulty was also caused by a disorder within the individual leader. This disorder had to be attended to as we dealt with other issues in the organization's life. The "boss" was so erratic and so powerful that the organization could not address any of the issues facing it until the leader calmed down.

Problem-Solving Approach. Other analysts pay attention to the problems the organization is facing. Most professionals in dispute resolution look at certain types of questions: What are the people fighting about? What decision needs to be made? Mediators want to know what the issue—the grievance—is. Does the problem have to do with safety, making a sale, electing a person to office? These kinds of questions get "solved" or "resolved" when the disputants come to an agreement or make a decision.

The problem with this method is that making a decision may not solve underlying problems, especially if the parties are not competent to carry out the decision, are angry, or remain antagonistic.

Churches often approach difficulties from this problem-solving perspective. They ask, "Are we clear about our goals? Do people agree on what the goals should be? Are 'they' committed to the organization's mission?" Or perhaps the members worry about whether they are doing things correctly—welcoming newcomers, inviting them to join, using appropriate liturgy or music to attract young people, and so forth. These approaches assume that if we can all agree on what to do differently, then the organization will improve, and the problem will be resolved.

Of course many problems can be solved this way. Organization Development, taught in many management schools, tends to focus on this dimension of organizational life, proposing collaborative problem-solving methods, addressing issues directly.

Systems Approach. A systems approach to organizational problems does not deny that difficulties can be caused by individuals and/or by problems the organization needs to address, but it also observes the reactive patterns or nonconscious agreements or "understandings" that people have about how they are supposed to act or how to get along. We will be using this approach exclusively in the Congregational Systems Inventory and the theory developed in this manual. This is not to imply that the other approaches are not valid and useful. The other approaches should also be considered when asking the question "What is going on in this organization?" Though we do not discuss the other approaches, do not assume they should be relegated to a low priority.

Homeostasis and Patterns

Built into the structure of the human being is a need[1] to be connected to others. Interaction makes families, clubs, lovers, teams, cliques, churches, mobs, businesses, and governments work; it's the basis of their very existence.

While in college I (Leas) observed a group gather every morning at the same place to wait for a bus. They usually arrived in the same order, stood in the same place, exchanged the same greetings, and boarded the bus in the same order. I can't imagine anyone told these people they had to behave in the same way each morning. Yet they did. Some of the patterns (or rules) may have been learned at home or school or by observing the behavior of others in similar situations: Ladies before gentlemen; older people sit, and younger people stand. Other patterns may have been worked out as the parties gathered at the same spot each day: Tom and Mary speak to each other; the others do not talk but simply acknowledge the presence of another with a nod of the head.

Anyone could give any number of examples of patterned behavior: Students often sit in the same seats in class; worshippers pray in the same pews; aerobic dancers have a penchant for the same spot on the exercise floor. But it's not just where one is placed that impacts what one does in relationships; individual people are given roles (and assume them). Certain activities are deemed appropriate for men (and not for women). Other activities are deemed appropriate for women only. Many of these patterns are rightfully criticized as sexist; they make it difficult for all people to have an equal and fair chance at employment, power, or to experience the joy of being eccentric.

Sometimes these expectations or role-rules have to do with one's tenure in the relationship, one's age, or one's assignments made as the relationship developed. In new work groups someone is expected to be the leader. There may not be an appointed or elected leader, but as the group gels, one person emerges as the responsible one, the one who thinks of what is needed for the group to function well, the one who invites people back into relationship, the one who smoothes over the conflicts, the one who indicates when it is time to leave. Of course not all of these roles have to be evident in one person. They can be shared or distributed within the group. Also, the same roles do not need to function in all groups. Some groups have gatekeepers; others do not. Some groups have clowns; others do not.

Systems theorists call this tendency of people in relationships to develop patterns and keep doing things in the same way "homeostasis." Once an organization or system gets in motion, it tends to keep going in the same way.

Think about the alternatives. If we could not depend on others to sit in the same place, follow our agreed-upon rules, and take various roles within the organization, it would require great time and energy to relate to or work with others. What would life be like if you didn't know which side of the bed was "yours"? If you didn't know what to expect when Mom comes home from work? Will you eat, do yard work, or have a fight?

Homeostasis is the tendency for a system, relationship, or organization to mold the behavior of others into predictable patterns, making it possible for us to "get along," to do work, to find safety, to trust. Without this tendency, every time we came together in a relationship we would have to invent the relationship over again.

Rigid Extremes. Getting fixed into rigid no-change relationships can be as problematic as being in flux about everything. In healthy relationships, either extreme—being too tight or too loose—for too long can be a serious problem. If we have no idea what is going to happen next, if we can't get dependable commitments to or from one another, then we have no system or organization. If we have too much order, too much dependability, too much status quo, then the organization will not adapt to changes in the environment; it will inhibit the growth and development of group members.

Indeed, an organization cannot grow if the homeostatic forces are totally in charge. Growth means that the system must accommodate newcomers, new patterns must develop as numbers increase, new adaptations must be made to changing environments, new agreements must be made as new personalities enter the system.

This tension or "pull" between chaos and homeostasis is important to a well-functioning system. When the relationship loses the ability to "lighten up" when appropriate or to "tighten up" when more order and control is needed, we say the system is "rigid." Rigidity can be either "overcontrolling" or "undercontrolling."

Systems and Codependence. Analysts sometimes refer to people in systems as being "codependent." This may refer to the cooperation within the system to keep it (or a person within it) functioning at one extreme end of the tight-loose spectrum. For example, a mother may "overfunction," when she does everything for everybody in the family: She does the meals, the laundry, the housekeeping, the nursing, the planning—everything—to such a degree the others rely on her to keep the system going. If Mom gets sick, the work stops or members of the family pressure her (and she pressures herself) to get the work done, or—instead of distributing the load in a just manner across all of the members of the family—the whole burden is placed on Dad or Sis who has to cover for Mom. So the pattern persists.

People often refer to a codependent relationship in terms of these tendencies to maintain extreme and unhealthy patterns. For many the word *codependent* means "inappropriately cooperative with overly rigid or overly loose behavior patterns." They may use the example of the alcoholic family where members discount, cover, minimize, hide, and deny the drunk's dysfunctional behavior: "Oh, he's much more pleasant to be around when he's had a drink," not acknowledging his inappropriate and damaging behavior.

But there's a problem with this definition of *codependent.* Such a definition assumes that the codependent is always functioning at the extreme tight end of the scale, needing to loosen up, be more differentiated, reduce dependence on another. Certainly such loosening may be needed, but not to the extent that one disengages or pulls out of the relationship.

Trying to deal with difficult behavior in a relationship, one can swing too far, saying, "Since we are overly dependent on each other, we break all dependency."

We do not think breaking all dependency is possible in a relationship. Every relationship is codependent to some degree or it is not a relationship. Every system is codependent to some degree or it is not a system.

Edwin Friedman writes about the need of leaders to differentiate themselves from the anxiety of the system, *while still staying connected.*[2] Of course that's the trick. If we leave, we have no system. If we leave for a short time and return but do not change our patterns, we obviously are not differentiated. We are still caught up in the patterns we have established for ourselves.

Formal, Informal, and Tacit "Agreements" in Systems

In his helpful book on systems Ken Mitchell discusses how patterns hold together in human relationships.[3] He says systems continue because of agreements or "contracts" people make with one another.

Sometimes the contracts are formal; these agreements we make with others are public and usually written. A church constitution is a formal contract. At least when the organization began or when the constitution was written, everyone knew that an agreement was taking place. Canon law is a formal contract, as are marriage vows (an agreement witnessed by others who will support the couple in holding to their vows). Job descriptions are formal contracts—written agreements about expectations: "If you do this, we will do that."

Other agreements are informal contracts. This is an understanding in which the parties are aware that a bargain is being made and communicate directly about what they are going to do or not do: "Would you mind picking up the kids on your way home from work tonight?" "No, I will be happy to do it." The agreement is verbal and may be public or private. Often staff meetings are a series of informal agreements (especially if no one keeps minutes). Staff members discuss what is needed, who is going to do what and when. This is informal contracting.

Mitchell calls a third kind of agreement "tacit." A tacit agreement has to do with the habits or patterns people establish as they interact over time. With no writing or clear discussion, expectations can develop. "That's my seat!" "You have always called when you were going to be out later than ten o'clock." Sometimes these expectations can be helpful, sometimes, not so helpful. An expectation that somebody is going to "mess up" can be a form of nonconscious contract: "I expect you will not get the book done on time, and sure enough, you don't."

Mitchell describes three categories of formal, informal, or tacit contracts: rules, roles, and rituals. We have added a fourth category: goals.

	FORMAL	INFORMAL	TACIT
RULES	By-laws Standard Operating Procedures	Special Cases Spoken guidelines "Crying babies go to nursery"	Norms Dress Codes Not talking about politics
ROLES	Pastor President Secretary	"I'm the devil's advocate." "I'm a pinch hitter."	Conflict Smoother Gatekeeper Matriarch Flack-catcher
RITUALS	Sunday Worship Induction Ceremony	Going out for ice cream after winning a game.	Greeting Rituals: Shaking hands "How are you?"
GOALS	Preach the word and rightly administer the sacraments	We need some new members around here	Let's grow old together

Figure 1
Examples of Contracts in Systems

Rules. Let's look at illustrations of each of these four categories, starting with *rules.*

Formal rules are easy to identify—laws, constitutions, and policies, for instance. They are written, public agreements that people have made about how they are going to make decisions, what is appropriate and inappropriate behavior, what time worship will be held, and so on.

Informal rules are agreements made about things on an ad hoc or temporary basis. "Please don't smoke in the house while the baby's here." "I am finding it difficult to make up my mind about which shirt to buy, will you make the decision for me?"

Tacit rules are silent agreements. Parties involved may not even be aware of the agreement. At our house we have a rule that people go to bed at 10:00 p.m. I don't recall ever having discussed this with anyone. Perhaps it was habit; perhaps that's when we all get tired; perhaps it was the practice in our families of origin; whatever, at ten we all go to bed. This does not mean that the rule can't be broken. Sometimes we break it to follow another rule: When we have visitors, we stay up later. Sometimes we break the rule to send a message to other family members: "I'm upset, so I am going to bed early." Or, "I'm upset, so I am coming to bed late." Or maybe, "I am very upset, so I am sleeping on the couch."

These tacit rules can be subtle, but they are known at some level. And the keeping or breaking of the rules influences the system as a whole. These rules are not invariable. Actually, they are modified from moment to moment, circumstance to circumstance. But when the rules are broken or changed, the system notices that something is out of balance and it will try to pull the people back into the previous patterns.

The following discussion is based on specific tacit rules discussed in *Facing Shame,* a book on family systems theory.[4] The rules represent a recurrent pattern that emerges as characteristic of a particular system. They describe behavior-influencing forces working within some families. The rules do not guarantee that a particular something will happen, but they indicate what is likely to occur in a given interactive system. They have both positive and negative qualities and can be particularly problematic if the systemic pattern fixes at the extreme tight-end or loose-end of a continuum.

Take the common rule: One must be in control of all behavior and interaction. This is a good rule—sometimes. Generally, out-of-control people are no fun to be around, but people who have to be in charge, not only of themselves but of others, can be a real pain.

When a system makes a strict rule, "The parents (or Dad) must be in control of the children's behavior and interaction," life can be most uncomfortable. If the rule is for the parent to take more control when anxiety arises, the family locks into rigid patterns of behavior as any crisis threatens.

Consider this continuum:

Controls Others <————————> Allows Others Freedom

The tacit rule about control (the place on this continuum at which the people in the system usually operate) is a problem when the group behavior stays at one place on the continuum and is unable to shift as the system requires it. For the infant, the parent must exercise more control than for the adolescent. But one hopes the tacit rule changes as the child —and the parent—mature. As a child enters adolescence, the application of family rules must change. Rigid control on the part of the parent often produces rigid rebellion in the child. Trying to get the patterns back to normal generally does not loosen the system but hardens it into dysfunctional coping patterns.

The problem is not always overcontrol; "undercontrol" can be as problematic. In some families the boundaries are too loose, "anything" goes. When a parent is unable to set limits, the child and family can experience abuse.

The issue of control is not just an issue between adults and children but can crop up between adults. Take the example of two women in a business partnership. They agree (formally and informally) that neither should be boss; their partnership will not be a hierarchical system. Each feels the other should be able to do what she feels appropriate when she feels it appropriate. Yet each partner comes to work only "when she feels like it." No one covers the phones. Sometimes neither is available to take a particular job. Each feels that the other is doing less then her share—but there is no way (in this system) to call each other to account. From a systems perspective, our concern is that the system stay "unstuck" and consider options. In the alcoholic family, members don't have options when there is always an identified patient. Even if a person stops drinking, the rest of the family may put pressure on that person to stay in the old patterns. In this case, the system is trying to stay in its rigid or dysfunctional pattern. Or when one stops drinking, another may take up the role of identified patient by acting out in some way.

Sometimes when attempting to make changes, the parties go from one extreme to the other. When this happens the various parties are merely switching roles; they are not changing the dysfunctional pattern. A responsible person might say, "Okay, if you are going to be irresponsible, I'll out-do you. I'll force you to be responsible by not doing anything at all."

Let's look at another family rule-continuum, this one having to do with perfection. Often this rule gets stated in terms of someone (I, you, we) always having to be "right." We must do the "right" thing. At face value, this is not such a bad rule. But when being perfect gets in the way of being human, being loving, allowing failure, then we are stuck at the rigid end of this continuum.

Be Perfect <————————> Don't Worry, Be Happy

One has a serious problem when the system is rigidly stuck at either end. Perfectionism often leads to loss of motivation, lack of risk taking, depression, workaholism, and denial of problems evident to others. The "don't worry, be happy" loose end of the spectrum can also lead to loss of motivation and lack of risk taking and effort, when being "laid back" reduces eagerness to take on a challenge or improve one's lot.

In a congregation that has a "be perfect" rule, members (and clergy) may continually bad mouth one another for imperfections in the worship service: The choir sang the anthem too slowly. The ushers weren't paying attention to the needs of members. The pastor didn't seem to deliver her message with precision and care. If the perfection rule is powerful, the choir might find a new director; the ushers might be removed; the congregation might call a new pastor. But the underlying problem will remain—rigid adherence to a rigid and "tight" rule.

Of course one needs to assess rules, problems, and systems carefully. The problem can be in the competence of one or more persons It can also be in the application of the rules or the rules themselves. It's usually a combination of these. Some novices in systems theory use the systemic dimension to discount their own or others' personal incompetence. When we ask about the ways rules function in the life of a system, we are considering only one of the many dimensions of what is going on in a relationship.

The other end of this perfection-continuum in a church system might mean that no one expects reliability or constancy in relationships. "We don't assume others will be reliable. What can you expect? They're just volunteers." With this "rule," poor, half-hearted performance is tolerated.

Though we won't delve into it, one more rule-continuum focuses on placing blame:

Find a Culprit <————> It Is Useless to Point Fingers

You might ask, "Why do you call these categories—control, perfection, blame—'rules'?" They are tacit rules when they govern our behavior, when they become standards against which we measure our success; they become "parent tapes" that try to regulate our behavior.

When looking at a system in terms of rules, we need to ask:

— Are we rigidly stuck at the loose end of the continuum?
— Are we rigidly stuck at the tight end of the continuum?
— If we are near the middle of the continuum, are we able to move to the right or left as appropriate?

Notice we are not trying to achieve a rule "balance"—always staying exactly in the center of the continuum. One must not just find the via media and stick to it. When you ride a bike, you have to lean a little to the left and then to the right.

Roles. Another kind of agreement made in the life of systems has to do with responsibility, i.e., who does what and how much authority is related to various tasks.

Formal roles are easy to identify: president, secretary, pastor, moderator. These are roles usually described in a constitution, book of order, canon law, or discipline. We acknowledge these roles as necessary for us to function as a certain kind of church.

Informal roles are usually established "on the spot" by mutual agreement. I used to belong to a congregation where no one ever scheduled who would usher on Sunday. We all knew that someone needed to do the task, but the job went to the person (over age ten) who arrived just a little bit earlier than the others.

Tacit roles are also powerful shapers of organizational life. Some people take on or are given roles necessary for the maintenance of life in that organization. I once belonged to a church where one member kept his eye on everything related to property and finances. He was not the treasurer. (I don't know if he ever had been.) He was not the chair of the buildings and grounds committee. (I don't know if he ever had been.) Nonetheless, he carried around a notebook that itemized all the tables, chairs, and desks in the church. He was always the one who added up the budget columns presented to the annual meeting to see if the total was correct. He kept an eagle eye on the use of fuel oil, the pastor's mileage, and the number of lights on in the building. Nobody had elected him to this role. No one had appointed him (as far as anyone could remember), but by common consent he was allowed to function as the steward of church resources and property.

Amazingly, when he left the church (at age sixty-five moving to the Sun Belt), it took hardly three months before another member had taken up this role—adding up the budget columns, keeping track of the building usage, making an inventory of church property. That congregation seemed to need a steward of church resources and property. When it was without one, it maneuvered another person into that position to fill the void.

I have noticed this same phenomenon with church-school teachers. For years a small church I pastored two Sunday-school teachers, one for the primary grades and one for middle-school grades. We regularly complained that we needed more teachers; we worried about having only two classes and each of those just a little too large. But try as we might we were never able to rope another person into the role of church-school teacher. Never, that is, until the older of the two teachers moved away. I thought we were down now to one teacher, but I was wrong. A person came forward to fill the position. It seemed the church believed it needed only two teachers. Was this a conscious decision? Definitely not. Consciously we tried and tried and tried to get more help. Nonconsciously we were probably sabotaging our efforts, making sure that we had enough help but not using more resources than the system believed it needed.

Sometimes people take on roles in the life of a system that are upsetting, stress producing, and (here's that word again!) dysfunctional. We've worked with organizations that seemed to need a person to take the blame for the group's problems—a person who doesn't seem to be holding up his or her end of the load, a person more ornery than most, a person who seems to receive the disapprobation of the others. Does any organization need to have an object onto which it can project the dark side of the people within it? Probably not universally, but that does seem to be the case in some relationships and in some organizations.

Sometimes people take on roles that every one agrees are pleasant, serviceable, and clearly functional to the health of the system. Often small congregations have people—usually not elected—who function as greeters, or gatekeepers, if you will. Prompted by personality type, the need of the system, or traditional roles that have emerged in the life of that system, an individual rises to the occasion and becomes the one who helps strangers feel welcome.

Rituals. Rituals are a third aspect of organizational life that impacts the way a system functions. Rituals help us get through transitions into and out of relationships, moving into new positions, recognizing changes that are taking place within the system or in the larger environment. Rituals help the system recognize the changes that are taking place in others. A wedding, for example, sends a message to the rest of the community that we should relate differently to those who are getting married. It is a means to help the system adjust to new roles, new realities.

But ritual is also a way that a system identifies itself. We are the people who do these rituals. A ritual helps maintain boundaries (who is in and who is out). Who is in? Those who know how to do these rituals. Who is out? Those who feel strange doing these rituals. It doesn't matter whether you have been an Episcopalian all of your life. If you go to another Episcopal church, you will probably feel like a stranger; that is, they will do the ritual there slightly differently than at your home church, and you will be a stranger until you learn to do the ritual as comfortably as the regulars do.

Formal rituals have long been part of church life. These are written in a prayer book, a bulletin, the hymnal, or distributed to congregations through denominational channels. Formal rituals are established over time and agreed on by the formal system. They include Sunday morning (or Friday night or Saturday morning) worship, funerals, weddings, prayer services, baptisms, confirmations, ordinations, investitures, etc.

Of course, formal ritual is not limited to the church. I am writing these words not long after the inauguration of Bill Clinton—clearly a formal ritual. Commentators watched and remarked on every move made, which Bible was used, the length of the address, where the president's spouse stood, on and on. In business, rituals are instituted for employees who retire or maybe for those who have been regular in their work for twenty years. Rituals are used at special times of the year to give bonuses, to recognize extraordinary gifts, or to make promotions, and to introduce new products.

Ritual can also be informal—such as celebrations of birthdays at the office; going out for ice cream after winning a softball game; a spontaneous demonstration in Times Square in celebration of a great national fete; a riot; or a protest march.[5]

Tacit rituals abound in church and out. They are the rites we engage in with little or no conscious awareness of what we are doing or why. Reciting a psalm-verse upon seeing snow-covered peaks at sunset, making the sign of the cross upon hearing of the death of a friend, shaking hands in greeting, waving in farewell—all are examples of rituals of which we are, for the most part, not conscious, unless someone does "it" wrong. Then we are aware that that person is not from our tribe, our system.

Goals. Mitchell does not talk about goals as a part of the contracting that goes on among members of a system. But we see this dimension as a profitable addition to his schema.

Formal goals include the statement of purpose, mission statement, or covenant that people write together to identify publicly who they are. Sometimes these are stated in a creed or affirmation of faith. Formal goals are also made by board members when they go on a weekend planning retreat and write their agreements on newsprint. They are formal goals because they are public, written, and agreed on in a process that is understood and endorsed by the people in the system.

Informal goals are those that emerge from a group's conversation about what they are going to do together. Staff meetings often result in informal goals. (If the staff keeps minutes of their meetings, they would be formal goals.) An example of an informal goal would be an agreement that people will all meet at the church on Saturday to clean up the tree blown over by the storm.

Tacit goals are those established through the agreements that people make nonconsciously about what they are trying to do. It is quite possible for an organization to have formal goals and tacit goals 180 degrees out of sync. A church's formal goal may be to bring Christ to the world, but the tacit goal may be for the parishioners to grow old together. If an organization's formal or informal goals contradict its tacit goals, the tacit goals will probably win out. The formal goals will be on paper; the tacit goals in people's hearts. This can be very confusing to new members or new pastors who actually believe what the organization has written on paper.

I knew a situation in which a pastor, when candidating to be the new minister of a congregation, asked the search committee and the congregation (in his candidating sermon) not to invite him to be the pastor unless they really wanted to change, especially to increase the number of those participating in worship. The search committee and the congregation assured him they were ready to grow. The pastor moved into the new setting and discovered their formal and informal agreements with him were not the same as the tacit agreement they had with one another about what would be required to grow as a congregation.

The new pastor believed that growth required new (to the congregation) music, a different music director, increased authority for the pastor, informal preaching, two Sunday worship services, and greater use of the building by community groups. In this situation, the congregation had a different "agreement" about worship, building use, and music, and the congregation's tacit goals about congregational growth were not the same as the formal and informal goals of the new pastor. Both parties felt they had not received what they had bargained for and finally agreed to part ways.

Seeing the Whole:
A Perceptual Shift for Congregational Leaders

Getting Past "My" Part of the Congregation

In his book *The Fifth Discipline,* Peter Senge describes an interesting learning disability in which it is difficult for people to appreciate what is happening in the larger system beyond "their" small part. For instance, often those in charge of the kitchen believe that the kitchen is there as a memorial to great cooks of the past; it is to be used only by "responsible" people; it is not to be used by teenagers or the uninitiated.

If one believes that one's part of the organization is the most important or finds it difficult (perhaps impossible) to empathize with the needs of other parts of the system, then it is very difficult for that person to work with (and for) others in the organization. It is not unusual for a pastor and the members of the Stephen Ministries team to believe that the care of souls is the number-one priority of the congregation. People committed to this work might discount the congregation's need for money, for a safe and secure building, or for fellowship groups.

But the same preoccupation can reside within trustees who see the congregation's first priority as making sure the bills get paid and the building does not fall down. Each party has minimal understanding or commitment to the goals of the whole and the needs of the other parts of the system.

This is not an unusual problem in businesses where one department believes that other departments don't understand its work; only if the work of "our department" is maximized can the organization move ahead. Marketing doesn't think research and development is realistic; manufacturing thinks marketing has no appreciation for the constraints manufacturing is under; and accounting believes that all departments (except accounting) are nearly out of control, spending beyond reasonable needs.

Seeing the Parts Related

To be realistic about the relationship of the parts to the whole, one cannot expect that the parts will think just about the good of the whole or that they will give appropriate weight in their deliberations to the needs of other parts of the system. Yet to the extent that the various parts can become more conscious of the needs of the others and of their own tendency to overvalue their own contribution, this learning disability can be minimized.

Thinking Systemically

Thinking systemically means that the parts of the whole take into consideration the needs of the other parts and the needs of the system as a whole. But there's more. Systemic thinking assumes multiple causes— not a simple cause; it assumes that there are many contributing factors to any given set of circumstances.

When there is tension in a congregation, there is usually a disagreement between the parties. As an example, let's say there is tension over this issue: "Be it resolved that this church use more popular music in the services of worship." The parties disagree over this resolution. But rarely is it only the substance of the disagreement that fuels the tension.

There are other questions: Who makes decisions about music? (Authority.) Are we becoming too informal? (Identity.) Do we really want new
people here—assuming new music will bring in new people? (Boundaries.)

Thinking systemically means seeing the multiplicity of causation.
Part of the cause of this congregation's tension might be the group's
"conflict rules" (don't talk directly with the person with whom you disagree) that interfere with the congregation's ability to make decisions.
Other causes may be particular personalities who exacerbate any conflict
because they are abrasive and authoritarian in style. Then also, there
may be historic tensions between the choir master and parishioners who
want to have a say in the music program. There might also be tension
arising from the different cultural realities experienced by people who
grew up during World War II and those who grew up in the sixties.
Their perceptions about appropriate music, worship, and ways to act
(especially toward one's elders) have distinctly different casts.

What then is the cause of the tension? Do we just need to have a
vote on the music? Can we negotiate a deal where we have two classical
hymns and one charismatic hymn per Sunday? Such decisions probably
wouldn't settle the dispute.

Only as the various parties can agree on what has led to the tension
can the tension be reduced. Does this mean that everything needs to get
worked through? No. Does it mean that certain "basic" issues need to
get worked through before the matter is "settled"? Probably not. The
way a system changes is for part of it to change. We change the part we
can. Then address other parts. The controversy never really ends.
Phases of it do. Pieces of it do. Some of it is addressed, but it is never
completely laid to rest. In the systems approach, we handle the parts we
can, knowing it will be inadequate and incomplete. When we change
any of the caused factors, it is likely we will impact every part of the
system.

S. L.

CHAPTER III

Creative Tension

Beyond Homeostasis

As we have noted in chapter I, congregations run the risk of becoming stuck in their successful strategies and overadapting until they are no longer able to respond to changes in their environment. What has worked well in the past becomes the mandate for the future. But this is the danger at only one end of a polarity.

There is another danger: too much change. In reacting to our "stuckness," we may swing to the other extreme. A congregation we visited recently had devoted major resources to small group ministry one year, to evangelism the next, to Stephen Ministries the next, etc. Stretched thin by multiple program experimentation, lay leaders were exhausted and coherent congregational direction was lost. When driven by trends or in ongoing efforts to respond to changing environments, congregations can lose their way, their identity, and their cohesiveness.

Congregations, like human beings, live between the polarities of order and freedom. Between these two fundamental requirements lies the stage upon which the history of the people of God has been played out. The tension between order and freedom has birthed the great stories of the Bible and framed the historical struggles of the church. The tension is reflected in the order and structure established in the Torah and the later response of the prophets who both embraced the Torah *and* pointed to the need for change. The tension is reflected again in the postexilic freedom symbolized by Ruth as a model of the new diversity within the people of God. The tension surfaced again when Jesus challenged the established rules about table fellowship and sought to enlarge the acceptable circle. The gospel of Matthew depicts Jesus as the embodiment of this very tension between order and freedom. Matthew's opening genealogy describes Jesus as both the son of David (connected to a history and a community) and the son of the new human being (a brand new person, free of the past). In this tension, the church continues to evolve and carry faith to new generations.

When congregations live between order and freedom, not allowing the excesses of either to dominate, an atmosphere is created in which different voices and approaches are honored. The tension becomes something life-giving, creative, and renewing, as the "internal variety" encourages the benefits of both order and freedom.

I (Parsons) know of a married couple that embodies this tension. She is a financial planner, willing to delay short-term gain to build long-term security. He is a financial risk-taker for whom the enjoyment of life is a high priority. Over the course of their marriage, one perspective has dominated the other from time to time, and excesses at either end of this polarity have brought hardship. His voice prevailed at times leading to the burden of debt. Sometimes her voice prevailed in ways that diminished their here-and-now enjoyment of life. But mostly their two differing perspectives live in tension with each other. The tension, comfortable at times, certainly does not exist in some kind of a "balance." But their willingness to bring their perspectives into ongoing dialogue has made it possible for them to weather economic changes and the typical crises of married life.

Organizational theorists describe this same tension as a "loose-tight paradox." Business organizations, for example, need to be able to orchestrate stable production and marketing functions as they remain flexible enough to move with the ever-shifting economic climate and market variables.

Family therapists also recognize this tension and describe it as an "integration-differentiation continuum."

Our very nature as humans calls us to be in relationships with others —a part of community—integrated into a human collective beyond ourselves. But our personal growth and maturity require that we differentiate ourselves from that community. At different points in our development, we may swing from one side of the polarity to the other, but it is in the tension between the two that we become fully human.

Because the forces of order and freedom are constantly in tension in congregational life, we would posit that healthy congregational systems will *create tension*—to maintain internal variety and stay flexible and open to renewal. Again, the healthy system moves along the continuum but is not stagnant and "balanced." A healthy congregation lives with certain kinds of contention created by the voices from both sides. We would argue that unless there are ongoing reasons for a congregational system to contend, unless there are opportunities to exercise these tensions, the congregation will lose its flexibility and experience decline. Without reasons to contend, congregations will either experience the excesses of order (which become overcontrol) or the excesses of freedom (which lead to chaos). One set of excesses is not preferred over the other. Either can kill a congregation.

Chaos and Overcontrol

As noted in chapter II, congregational leaders can be unaware of the nature of their particular congregational system and unable to evaluate how effectively they are managing the order-freedom tensions. On the "order" side, poorly managed tension can lead to brittle or stuck congregations. On the "freedom" side, it can lead to disengaged or unconnected congregations. We have noticed that many congregations can exhibit some excesses on both sides at the same time; it is possible for a congregation to be rigid in some respects and chaotic or unconnected in others. But a congregation that is unaware of the excess (or loss of tension) may in fact treat the excess as the status quo or desired state.

As consultants much of the conflict we address is sparked by an effort to move a congregation out of an institutionalized excess. For example, we often enter a congregational system that has excessively concentrated authority in a small group of people. This group, though it may not be on the official church board, can informally control decisions and discourage participatory decision making. This excess of authority is often accepted as "the way things are." Pastors who survive in such a system learn to adjust to the power group. People unconsciously defer to the group and consult it about possible decisions. This excess becomes the status quo and the organization resists changing it. But often new members entering the system become tired or frustrated with this arrangement and act to challenge the concentrated authority. Conflict begins, in this case as an effort to regain a healthy tension by more broadly dispersing authority and widening participation in decision making.

Congregational Systems Inventory Measures Degree of Tension

The Congregational Systems Inventory measures the approximate degree of tension in a number of areas in a congregation's life. A loss of tension indicated by very high or very low scores on the inventory will suggest needed change in the life of a congregation. We will note, for example, that congregations that have abandoned the orderliness of good planning in favor of freedom will likely face ongoing conflicts focused on the setting of priorities and the selection and evaluation of pastoral leadership. We see congregations that are not clear about their identity and direction as being more conflicted and repeatedly so.

Because there is no balance, only tension, we are unable to posit neat formulas by which congregations can remain vital and effective in the decade ahead. We are not putting forth a neat or tidy proposition but hope that the CSI will point to (1) the wisdom and value of good tension between polarities and (2) the importance of maintaining internal variety. We hope it will help congregational leaders develop a consciousness about the nature of the system within which they minister.

G. P.

CHAPTER IV

Systems Dimensions

Introduction

Because our congregational assessment approach has been shaped by systems theory (open or family systems) and by recent literature from the "organizational architecture" field, we could address and emphasize any number of organizational dimensions, including the unwritten rules or norms that guide behavior in a system or the many programmatic aspects of parish ministry. But we have selected six dimensions—on seven scales—that parallel the Seven S framework developed by Richard Pascale and his colleagues.[1] These six dimensions encompass both key organizational functions and the way people function in church life. They address some of the pivotal structural and leadership dimensions that most clearly describe the organizational dynamics shaping a congregation's ministry.

Strategy

Definition

Strategy is the way congregations put their vision into practice. This dimension, which might also be called planning or mission, assesses the congregation's attitude toward the future. It places the congregation on a continuum between rigidly planning for the future and being utterly spontaneous—freely responding to the present. As is the case with every dimension in this material, some degree of each polarity is necessary and both are equally valued.

A *planned* strategy enables a congregation to develop a clear sense of purpose and direction. This discernment of direction, usually developed through some evaluation process of the congregation's strengths and resources in relationship to its opportunities for ministry, will generate a set of goals and a practical agenda intended to help the leadership achieve those goals. A planned strategy brings organizational criteria to bear on the evaluation of ministry. Because we know where we are heading and what we are trying to accomplish, we are in a position to say more clearly whether our resources and leadership talent are being well-used.

A *spontaneous* strategy allows a congregation to maintain an openness to God's leading (to the movement of the Spirit), recognizing that we cannot see into the future or anticipate completely the changes and opportunities of the future—within or beyond the congregation. A congregation's ability to sit loose in the saddle and remain responsive to emerging opportunities and needs can offset a tendency to overcommit to plans; it helps avoid the blinder effect created by excessive planning. If change is to be a constant in life and surprises are the expected reality, a disciplined attitude of flexibility and openness will be essential for future congregational vitality and effectiveness.

Excesses at the Planned End of the Scale

In this dimension when tension is lost at the planned end of the scale, the effects will become evident. (These excesses are infrequent in our sample because most voluntary systems do not overplan.) When these excesses develop, planning becomes an end in itself. When planning activities are done for their own sake, people confuse the planning process with effective implementation; they spend an inordinate amount of time and energy tending to the plan. There may be comfort and security in the process, but the planning becomes the end rather than the means.

While effective planning gives a congregation a lens through which to look at the surrounding world, overreliance on a planned strategy prevents leaders from seeing other options and opportunities. Extensive planning filters out issues and possibilities that don't fit into the plan.

This blinder effect discourages people with new or different ideas. Creative proposals are rejected because they lie outside the field of vision created by excessive planning. If a congregation has elaborate plans to develop a new facility and add new members, and the planning is rigidly applied, those who value ministry to the community or the congregation's involvement in regional mission will be shut out or ignored. In addition, those who see opportunities to respond immediately to needs within the congregation are discouraged from acting on their ideas.

We have worked with a congregation that exhibited most of the characteristics of excess at the planned end of the scale. This congregation had honed management-by-objectives to a fine art. The church set clear, specific, manageable goals at an annual retreat of the board. They not only set goals, they also checked their progress on each at the end of the year. But the setting and evaluation of goals became the focus of the church. The congregation was unable to see that staff relationships were in a shambles; the leadership was so caught up in managing the plan that they were unable to address anything that could not be quantified and achieved within a year.

Leaders came to understand that success meant reaching one's goals. So each year they set goals that were lower than the previous year, and most of those goals were irrelevant to the quality of congregational life. The church became more focused on its goals than on getting work done, and the staff became more and more uptight and burdened with reaching the goals. Because of the need to look good on paper, secrecy increased, candor decreased, especially among the staff. They had become captive to their planning process, which encouraged them to do less rather than more and helped them avoid their reasons for being a church.

Excesses at the Spontaneous End of the Scale

When tension is lost at the spontaneous end of the scale, one sees an equally difficult set of characteristics. In church life these excesses are more common than planned excesses. Why? Some theological positions take a dim view of planning; volunteers often have little enthusiasm for planning; and many leaders have noticed that the most elegant planning processes can be neutralized by either the momentum of past practice or the inertia often associated with voluntary systems.

We have seen many churches at this end of the scale. The excess, in fact, is endemic in mainline congregations. These churches set goals at a planning weekend and never look at them again. At the next year's planning retreat, the process begins right where it did the year before. The newsprint record of the visioning process is rolled up and stored in a corner of someone's church office. Veteran leaders learn to distrust planning efforts or to endure them as opportunities to build relationships with no expectation that plans will be implemented.

Churches that have never seriously planned find themselves in a predicament when they search for a new pastor. Because the church is not clear about who it is and where it is going (and it would take a long time to figure it out), the board leaves that task to the search committee; a small group is allowed to establish the church's goals and vision. It is not uncommon, for example, for a search committee to conclude that a congregation is ready to commit to a major growth process. The search committee then will look for a pastor who can fill this bill. When she is hired, however, much to the committee's disappointment, many people are dissatisfied, "growth" never having been a priority for them.

Without understanding and gaining agreement about the goals of the church, the church will find itself in painful and repetitive conflict.

The varied expectations parishioners have for clergy and program create a significant managerial task for the congregational leaders. We have observed that spontaneous systems in excess prevent leaders and parishioners from bringing clear organizational criteria to bear on the evaluation of clergy and the overall ministry. Without the organizational yardsticks born of good planning, the system is open play for many competing and conflicting personal criteria; every parishioner knows what a pastor is supposed to be and do.

When the church does not have a clear plan that sets purpose and direction, smaller groups and individuals are left to discern direction for themselves. Congregational projects can become disconnected from one another. Individual programs and groups can develop their own direction (often tacitly) in isolation from the work of the board or other groups. This can lead to redundant or conflicting efforts. If these disconnected efforts become entrenched, efforts to produce a coherent plan will be resisted, and turf wars can follow.

Spontaneous systems tempt leaders to be consumers of current trends and fads. A congregation can grasp for packaged programs and strategies that promise congregational rejuvenation. Usually these efforts are short-lived. We have seen congregations focus on small-group ministry one year, a new evangelism strategy the next, and new-member ministry the next—without any clear rationale or sequence to their efforts.

Living in the Tension

A congregation that takes both poles of this dimension seriously can maintain a healthy tension between good planning and an openness toward new opportunities for ministry. This tension is sometimes uncomfortable, especially if the leadership is willing to honor both the voice for planning and the voice for flexibility. At some points in a congregation's life, one emphasis will appropriately have priority over the other. But when they are in dialogue with each other, the congregation is likely to have a clearer direction and know its goals and priorities. It will be able to encourage creative initiative, ongoing visioning activity, and a spirit of openness toward new possibilities. Living in the tension in this dimension makes it possible for a congregation to plan for surprises—plan with flexibility.

One congregation that maintained this tension created a thorough, in-depth, long-range plan approximately every four years. It also did an annual planning update that included a "what if?" revisioning process, encouraging leaders to consider new directions for ministry. A small portion of the budget was set aside annually for research-and-development-type experiments. The board members were required to participate in some annual exploration of the needs of the community, thereby staying in touch with changes in the environment. Also an annual award was given to the lay leader with the most creative new program idea.

Authority

Definition

Authority is the ability to influence decision making in the congregation.
The poles of this dimension describe the extent to which authority is
concentrated in the hands of a few people or dispersed to larger groups or
the entire congregation.

Concentrated authority may refer to the authority given by a role
(formal, informal, or tacit) that has the right to make decisions or act on
the behalf of others. But this is not the only kind of authority exercised
by people in organizations. A consultant or fund raiser may be carefully
listened to and her advice taken very seriously, even though she has not
been authorized by the congregation or the board to make decisions.
Perhaps you know of church members to whom people look for information, wisdom, or guidance. This may be because they have been doing a
certain job for a long time or clearly have competencies in a certain area
of the parish life. This is a kind of authority, an authority that comes
from ability.

The authority that comes from ability can be diminished when
people have a short tenure in roles and are unable to learn their craft well.
For example, if people are asked to teach church school, but only for
three months, or on the first Sunday of every month, they are less able to
become expert, less able to develop relationships, less able to develop a
sense of competence. Consequently, they will probably have less authority than someone who has been trained and has taught church school
regularly for several years. When a person has both expertise in the field
and is given a role of authority (for example, an expert teacher is made
church-school superintendent), the organization can become dependent
on that concentrated authority.

Congregations that have concentrated authority have a number of
advantages over those whose authority is more dispersed. It is usually
easier and faster to make decisions when authority is concentrated because not many people have to be consulted. Concentrated leadership is
generally more decisive and more consistent. Those most experienced at
the work are most likely to be making the decisions.

When referring to *dispersed* authority, we are pointing to decision

making that is distributed among a number of people. Baptist and congregational churches tend to have more dispersed formal systems of
governance than do Episcopal or Methodist congregations. Congregational systems often have larger boards, bicameral leadership (deacons
separated from trustees), and insist that issues (such as approval of the
church budget) affecting a large number of members be taken to the
congregation for review and approval. In a more concentrated system
such as the Episcopal Church, the vestry may not take the congregation's
budget to the congregation for approval.

There are some advantages to having more dispersed authority.
People are usually less resistant to ideas they have had a chance to shape.
When they feel they were not a part of the decision, they tend to be less
committed and contribute less than they would have if they had been
given an opportunity to say no or to revise the decision.

When it comes to the "experience and expertise" dimension of
authority, a congregation is more likely to put new people into leadership
when dispersal of authority is a systemic requirement. Years ago being
elected to an Episcopal vestry was a "life" term—unless you chose to
resign. New blood on the board was rare, often concentrating authority
in the hands of the old-timers. In congregational systems where board
members are required to take regular sabbaticals (you may not serve on
the board after a three-year term, without a year off), the congregation
generally has more dispersed authority than where people are able to
succeed themselves year after year. (*Nota bene*, there is no guarantee
that authority will be dispersed when the organization rotates members
off boards; as we all know, sometimes a clique will share leadership
roles; sometimes spouses succeed each other on the board, keeping the
authority concentrated in certain families.) Church requirements—according to the by-laws or by tradition—to find new leadership at regular
intervals can help disperse authority and pressure the system to encourage more grassroots involvement in decision making.

Excesses at the Concentrated End of the Scale

When tension is lost in this dimension toward the concentrated end of the
scale, several organizational difficulties can be experienced. When
individuals or small groups have the power to derail leadership decisions,

others within the organization can be terribly demotivated. One may feel, *If I have no impact on the decision, why bother participating at all?* In systems where small numbers of people can sabotage the work of others—not responding to their needs and interests—it is common for those whose work has gone for naught to quit, pull back, or rebel. Many a petition for dismissal has been circulated by people who felt their ideas and proposals were not taken seriously.

When power groups become entrenched and dominate others and the narrow self-interests of the in-group regularly prevail at the expense of other interests, congregational morale will decline and enthusiastic participation wane.

In organizations where authority is rigidly concentrated, leadership tends to be recycled, excluding new people. People in power do not want to give it up. Keeping control seems appropriate because it is the pattern and because the "leaders" believe themselves to be the experts; others with less experience and training will not be as well informed and will not make appropriate decisions. This, of course, leads to the phenomenon of in-groups and out-groups, which often means that energy is wasted on unnecessary competition.

In systems of concentrated authority we have noticed that people with authority often become blind to their impact on others. They don't see how demeaning it is not to have your ideas taken seriously. Indeed, it is difficult for them to notice they are not taking an idea seriously, as they can give a reason for discounting it: "We tried that in 1958 and it didn't work then; I doubt that it will work now."

Concentrated authority can take various forms in congregational life. Here are two examples.

One congregation started in the early sixties, led by a dynamic and effective pastor. People respected and admired him greatly. He loved his role as the expert on how to "do church." No decisions were made without first coming to him for approval. No one would think of doing something at the church without his involvement and blessing. Committees were always small, usually the same people serving year after year on a certain committee. Committee members did not rotate each year, so it was not possible to get people off boards unless they offered to step down. If people did not like the style of the pastor or the activities of the church, they were not without choices: they could acquiesce or leave.

Another congregation—in Southern California: those who were

enamored by the small-group approach to ministry had run the church for years. Budget decisions were shaped around the importance of small-group ministry. New members were welcome if they were interested in small-group participation. Despite the fact that the neighborhood had an influx of younger families that had little time for small-group meetings and found their social life elsewhere, the power elite insisted that the congregation continue in that direction. Attendance waned, enthusiasm dwindled.

Excesses at the Dispersed End of the Scale

In recent years it has been popular to decry the evils of hierarchy and extol the virtues of collaborative decision making. Each, however, can be appropriate depending on the circumstances.

When it is not clear who holds authority, people can be confused about who makes the decisions, or whether they will get made.

Too many powerful boards can disperse authority. We recently worked with a congregation that had three major boards: deacons, trustees, and an executive committee. Each thought it was the final authority. Each thought it was responsible for initiating and funding programs and protecting the congregation from the vagaries of those who seemed to have only their self-interests in view. Conflict that hindered the work of the church made it difficult to get anything done.

Authority can also be dispersed as leaders are rotated too often; this discourages the development of competency. In one church a new social action committee was appointed each year. (This was not the policy of the church, but it was their practice.) Each year people who were new to the idea of social action, naive as to the impact of their ideas, and uncertain about which areas of concern to address would sit down and attempt to figure out what they were supposed to do and how to do it. Their efforts were always feeble and their impact on the congregation minimal. If the members of this committee had known they were going to be involved for a while, they could have in time developed some competency, their confidence would have improved, and they would have been a more powerful (authoritative) force in the organization. A congregation that does not encourage competency development is not likely to get effective leadership.

Congregations with a rigid (excessive) commitment to dispersed leadership tend to distrust those who are given formal leadership roles. This is a "chicken and egg" problem. It is difficult, if not impossible, to tell whether the distrust of leadership comes from the dispersed authority or the dispersed authority comes from the distrust of leadership. The impact of not being able to move out of this behavior can have serious debilitating consequences. For example, in one presbytery we've seen a concerted concern that someone will "do something" to damage the total organization. Because of this, observers sit in on most committee meetings. Decisions that could have been in the purview of one committee must be evaluated by other committees and then approved by the entire presbytery before action can be taken or the policy installed.

This kind of a problem also draws out the decision-making process. Not only are decisions complicated, they cannot be made expeditiously.

When one discovers that decisions are regularly challenged and gone over again and again by different levels of the organization, one is not motivated to lead. Volunteers say, *This isn't worth it. Such ponderous ways of making decisions are not a good use of my time.*

Another problem noted by many behavioral scientists is that consensus decisions are more likely to get lowest common denominator results. Instead of striving hardest for excellence, the organization and the people in it strive to get the decision made. Getting a decision is more important than what the decision is. The need for closure pushes so hard on the group that members lose patience with what is being worked on and quit worrying about what solution is chosen. We have experienced negotiations that, after dragging on and on, reached the point where people no longer felt motivated to hang on to their original principles and values. Their new value became "How can we get this over with?"

We worked with one United Church of Christ congregation in excess at the dispersed end of the authority scale. Here board members rotated their committee assignments each year. It did not matter whether you knew (or cared) anything about missions or education; you could well be assigned as chair of that committee at the beginning of the year. Chairs were new each year so no one became entrenched in a fiefdom. No members developed any real competency or commitment to a project in the church. Indeed, this church actually discouraged people from showing any real competency. At periodic events that honored the leaders of the church, care was taken to make the speeches brief to emphasize the egalitarian spirit and the democratic process.

No one was to stand out or lead, including the pastor. All decisions were to be made by consensus. Without full agreement of all parties, no decisions were made. That meant that strong pressure was put on people to get with the program or not voice their disagreements. The press for consensus resulted, almost always, in choosing the lowest common denominator. This church lost members who lacked the patience to endure processes that emphasized consensus, and it lost the gifts of specially talented people who stood out from the group.

Living in the Tension

Between each of the excesses, concentrated and dispersed authority, we are not looking for a balance; the balance cancels out the tension between the values at either end of a polarity. Rather, we are looking for the ability to move back and forth, sometimes experiencing dispersed authority, sometimes experiencing concentrated authority. The issue is not "Can we get the right mix every time we have a decision?" but, "What is right for this situation—hierarchical decision (as in the case of deciding how to approach the repair of a malfunctioning computer—call in the expert) or a consensus decision (as in the case of needing ownership and high commitment from all parties) or a mixture of consultation with experts and hierarchical decisions? Congregations that are able to live in the tension can choose different types of decision making depending on the issue at hand. They are not stuck with only one approach.

A large Presbyterian congregation with four staff clergy, five professional laypeople (a religious education director, a director of the day care and nursery school, a counselor, an office manager, and a music director) demonstrates how to work with this tension. This church was working with us on the question of how much authority the senior pastor should have for making decisions relating to the work of the staff. Should each staff person have to come to the senior pastor for approval of any project before it was undertaken? To what extent should the senior pastor consult with the staff as a whole, several departments, or the work of one staff person? Are there any areas of work that should regularly be the purview of the entire staff, or just the clergy, or just those who work with education?

We recommended that the staff consider differentiating among the types of decisions made and establishing criteria for choosing when decisions would be made by consensus, when they would be made by the person responsible for the work, and when there would be consultation with the senior pastor, who would make the final decision. By consensus (that is, through the use of dispersed authority) the staff team called for consensus decision making on certain issues (1) that affected the whole staff, (2) on which there needed to be high commitment, and (3) on which there needed to be significant input from all parts of the organization. Unless there was substantial conflict within the staff on the issue, and, after several serious attempts to work the conflict through, the staff was unable to arrive at consensus, the senior pastor would not be the final authority on issues such as establishing the goals of the staff team, agreeing on the staff's corporate prayer and worship life, and determining which decisions are collaborative and which are hierarchical!

The staff also agreed that some decisions needed to be hierarchical, and others should be hierarchical after consultation with the people affected by the decision or with experts on the subject. The staff agreed that the senior pastor would have final authority to decide the preaching schedule for the clergy, but that they would be consulted as a group before the final decision would be made about who preached and when.

This differentiation of uses of authority did not stop at neatly pigeonholing all decisions into clear categories. The staff recognized that there were times when the general rule, "This is a consensus decision," or, "This is a decision that will be made by a staff vote," or, "This is a decision to be made by the department chair," could be challenged or changed to fit variable circumstances.

On one occasion the senior pastor felt that, though the staff had agreed that hiring decisions were to be the senior pastor's (after consultation with the staff), this particular decision needed the wholehearted commitment of the whole. So he made this hire a collaborative decision.

Sometimes the staff would say, "We don't want to make this particular decision collaboratively." And sometimes the staff said, "This particular issue needs to be opened up to fuller staff discussion and involvement than our agreed upon structure ordinarily called for." So the decision rules were not set in concrete. They were not rigid, nor were they nonexistent so that folks had no idea what might happen from one moment to the next.

This pattern can also be instituted in the relationship between the pastor and the church board or between the board and the congregation. The constitution or canon law or the discipline may say that the church board has the right to make decision a or decision b, but the board may choose to open the decision to the larger congregation to get its understanding and commitment. In such a case the board and congregation should have the same kind of clarity and tension evidenced in the multiple staff team above. If the board always goes to the congregation for decisions the board should be making, there is a problem. On the other hand, if the board never goes to the congregation for consultation (indeed collaboration), then there's a problem at the other end of the polarity.

Process

Definition

The *process* scale measures both the information-sharing and decision-making procedures in a congregation. To what extent are these procedures clearly defined and regulated or variable and left to the discretion of individuals? Both poles—having clear operational maps and encouraging individual freedom—are equally desirable in congregational life.

A *mandatory* process provides clear organizational maps or guidelines. Decision-making procedures have been defined and communicated so that people and groups know how and where they can influence (or make) decisions. Boards and committees know whom to consult and whom to inform during the course of their deliberations. This clarity extends to handling conflict and solving problems. People know where to take complaints and what conflict management processes to follow.

Providing this kind of definition frees people from unneeded ambiguity or confusion regarding decision making and gives needed self-definition to the many entities within a system. Those in leadership roles know the range of their own authority. They have job descriptions that define the scope of their responsibility and mechanisms whereby they can evaluate their work. These processes, because they are mandated, reduce the tendency to create personality-dependent leadership roles or positions. New leaders can move into established positions and continue the work with little disruption. People can assume leadership positions with a realistic picture of what is expected because they are entering charted territory.

Mandatory processes link or connect and coordinate the parts of the system. Committees also have job descriptions that help them place their work within the larger context of the congregation's ministry. Among committees and staff, information-sharing needs are defined. For example, education, worship, and new member ministry functions know when to talk with the others and how to get the information they need to do their part in relation to one another.

A system that values *discretionary* processes encourages individual initiative in terms of problem solving and seeks to avoid undue constraints that create dependency. Leaders are able to use their own judgment more often and within their own areas of ministry, they can create guidelines suitable to their leadership styles and the needs of the people with whom they work. The chair of an evangelism committee can work with that committee to define processes for making decisions and coordinating the work. Members of the committee are free to develop more effective or imaginative ways to communicate with other related groups in the congregation. People can spend less time worrying about policy and procedure and focus on the work of ministry.

Discretionary systems encourage people to move beyond the law and focus on grace. The operational life of the congregation is better able to honor differences in leadership style and philosophy of ministry. People are rewarded for using their gifts creatively and accepted with their differences.

Another benefit of discretionary processes is that they help congregations respond more flexibly to changing circumstances. Changes in the shape of a congregation's ministry require adaptable operational processes. We see this often in congregations that are moving from one size to another.

Excesses at the Mandatory End of the Scale

When tension is lost at the mandatory end of the scale, processes created to define decision making, information sharing, accountability, or conflict management become heavy and burdensome. Policies and procedures lack freeing definitions and good connections; they rigidly constrain people.

When mandatory process is in excess, the system is preoccupied with the rules and with following the process at all costs. Monitoring compliance with policy takes up disproportionate amounts of time and energy. Policies intended to save time and give form to the work become an end in themselves as boards spend more and more time in legalistic discussions about by-laws, accountability, and using proper channels.

This excess discourages risk taking. New ideas that do not come through the appropriate channels are rejected. Decision-making processes tend to be slow because the bureaucracy mandates that all hoops be cleared. Creative people withdraw under these circumstances or produce underground efforts to by-pass the procedural morass.

One congregation had very clear operating procedures for all aspects of church life. Every leader in every committee knew his place, responsibilities, and authority. People rarely had questions about who was supposed to do what or when. The board had developed a very large and complete *Operating Procedures Manual* kept in three-ring binders so that new policies could be added.

But this church was obsessed about whether people were following the rules. They had difficulty adapting to changing situations (such as people not fulfilling their responsibilities or not following the rules). The pastor paid a heavy price in terms of stress. He was expected to monitor the rules and help everyone follow the map, and ended up in a position of overcontrol. It was very difficult to experiment with new ideas or programs because of the barriers created by policies. This rigidity spilled over into other aspects of the church's life, suppressing freedom and the possibility of creativity that comes with it.

Excesses at the Discretionary End of the Scale

When tension is lost at the discretionary end of the scale, an equally destructive picture will emerge. Since roles and responsibilities are not well defined, people don't know how to function relative to the rest of the organization. The parts become disconnected for lack of good information flow. Leaders develop a compartmentalized view of their work and don't see the overall picture. Tasks agreed to by the board or congregation go undone because no process exists to assign, track, or evaluate the work of ministry.

Discretionary systems in excess create confusion about turf. People will inadvertently make decisions or take actions that threaten or challenge another individual or group. We see this frequently around the use of memorial funds when their use is undesignated and the process for deciding when to use them is unclear. Excessive discretion in the system encourages power struggles focused on who has the right to do what.

This excess also creates an environment conducive to dysfunctional conflict behavior. In the absence of good conflict management processes, people invent their own. Conflicts are often driven underground because people don't know how to address them directly. Tacit conflict rules kick in to fill the vacuum leading to triangulation, gossip, and back-biting.

One congregation that lived in a discretionary excess had a building that was a mess, embarrassing to walk in to. When people wanted to find materials, they had no idea where to look. Frequently members, clergy, or officers could not find keys to unlock rooms or closets and sometimes would find themselves locked out of the building prior to an evening meeting.

Members in this church did not know what the various committees were doing. Committee meetings often lacked agendas and wandered off task, meeting late into the evening. Sometimes committees decided to do things beyond their own budget limitations or against the basic norms of that denomination. But those who recognized these problems had no idea how to tell these committees that they were off base.

Living in the Tension

A congregation that takes both poles of this dimension seriously, will keep a healthy tension between operational maps and individual freedom. Advocates for strong policy and advocates for individual initiative will remain in dialogue, recognizing that, at a given moment in the life of a congregation, a greater need may exist to emphasize one polarity more than the other.

We have worked with a congregation that exhibited this tension in a number of ways. Members as well as lay and clergy leaders had clear guidelines for handling problems and complaints, but room was allowed for individual discretion. Their policy was to go directly to the person with whom you have a complaint, but they recognized that sometimes an intermediary step would be needed. Discussion of existing policies and procedures was encouraged. People were expected to follow those policies but with some flexibility.

In that congregation, committees and work groups established job descriptions that set forth how that committee was to communicate with others and how it should make decisions. Yet these policies were reviewed periodically. Leaders were trained to conduct effective, efficient, and user-friendly meetings.

Pastoral Leadership

Definition

Pastoral leadership is the way the pastor goes about generating intended change in the church system. Pastors function on a continuum between managerial and visionary, between coping with complexity and coping with change, between organizing and motivating. Both poles of this leadership dimension are necessary and valuable in congregational life.

Managerial pastors are keenly aware of the current needs of the congregation and organize resources to address those needs. They value a congregational plan that states goals clearly and connects program priorities to budgetary realities. They organize people toward those goals and guide others to do systematic problem solving. Managerial pastors invest themselves in producing practical results through step-by-step effort that is sensitive to power issues and potential conflicts. They recognize the importance of realistic timetables for getting things done and tend to focus on what can be accomplished this year.

Transformational pastors is focus on future possibilities and invest energy in shaping a vision for that future. These pastors work to inspire others in order to create change. They point to a larger and longer-term picture of the congregation's mission and are willing to take risks to introduce the changes necessary to achieve that mission. Transformational pastors enroll others in their vision and create work teams that are enthusiastic about overcoming the obstacles to change. They continually speak to future possibilities and tie their vision to the congregation's values.

Excesses at the Managerial End of the Scale

When tension is lost at the managerial end of the scale, pastors overfocus on the control of the resources and programs. This tunnel vision obscures the need for significant change or for a longer-term view of the congregation's purpose and direction. Leadership energy is excessively focused on control, e.g., reducing organizational risks, making sure the budget is kept, and keeping track of time and property.

Pastors managing in excess focus on this year's goals and objectives and this month's program development to the exclusion of longer-term issues. An excessive focus on short-term events blinds the pastor to the effects of longer-term changes and to the need for discontinuous change. These pastors put the bricks in place one at a time when circumstances suggest that they need to redesign the house.

Managerial pastors prefer planned strategies. They are at their best when they can align the resources to meet clear goals. But when managerial leadership is used excessively, the pastor will overcommit to the plan and discard ideas or information that hasn't been run through the planning process. In excess, they don't know what to do with transformational lay leaders or staff members and have trouble using transformational talent.

We have worked with a pastor who helped his congregation maintain balanced budgets and who recruited enough people to fill the vacancies each year. He followed through with planning efforts, especially to reach short-term goals. In the meantime, his congregation, while effectively managed, continued to decline in Sunday attendance, pledging units, and overall vitality. Part of this decline was the result of changes in the community and especially in the neighborhood that had aged in recent years and become more commercially developed.

The changes necessary to counteract these trends required a level of risk and vision and probably a number of discontinuous changes that the pastor could not introduce through the incremental improvements of managerial thinking. This pastor, caught in a managerial excess, eventually concluded that the congregation could not get there from here.

Excesses at the Transformational End of the Scale

When tension is lost toward the transformational end of the scale, pastors overestimate the congregation's ability or willingness to change. Roy Oswald has noted that in the first year of a new pastorate many clergy are tempted to introduce changes before they have deepened their relationship with the congregation. Speed Leas' most recent research on clergy firings indicates that most clergy get in trouble within their first two years. Some of this difficulty clearly reflects transformational excesses whereby the pastor is overfocused on a change agenda.

Transformational leadership in excess disregards practical issues. Administrative and organizational details are ignored as the pastor pushes toward a visionary goal. The oversight of institutional needs is ignored or delegated to others without follow-up.

When change is introduced without an accompanying effort to provide structure to handle the change, the congregation moves toward chaos. Time-tested strengths may be abandoned and the congregation's purposes and identity will become fragmented or obscured. New programs and directions for ministry are transitory. Like individuals who become overwhelmed with change, congregations will also suffer from structure loss and become vulnerable to internal conflict. Pastors who exhibit these excesses are also vulnerable because they lose touch with the core values of the congregation and lose connection with those they are trying to lead. Pastors who challenge the accepted way of doing things leave the impression they do not value what others have done before. The pastors vision becomes detached from the values and history of the congregation and loses its ability to generate enthusiasm.

We worked with a pastor who introduced one idea after another, building coalitions around these ideas. The program efforts of the congregation became more and more fragmented as new projects unfolded. New endeavors in evangelism and small group ministry were understaffed and underfinanced. Lay leaders felt unsupported or eventually burned out. The pastor by that point had moved on to another project and had abandoned the previous two. The pastor also began to complain that people weren't really committed and that he was casting pearls before swine. Board members began to anticipate the pastor's lack of attention to budgeting and other administrative details. They prepared to counter him at every meeting. The pastor felt betrayed by a group of people whom he thought had been "really ready to establish a new direction for this church."

Living in the Tension

Pastors have several choices about how they can live in tension between these two valued ways of leading. Some pastors work to develop both sets of characteristics within themselves. They learn to lead with vision but to manage the vision. Some, having strong leanings (by temperament or education) toward one pole, seek continuing education offerings to reclaim the skills and sensitivity of the other side.

Another option for pastors is to team up with others who function from the opposite pole. Transformational pastors may intentionally select managerial staff members or seek out managerial lay leaders to provide ongoing counsel. In these cases, maintaining an open and enduring dialogue is critical for the maintenance of a healthy tension.

We know an Episcopal rector who, because of his own strong transformational leadership tendencies, consistently selected managerial senior wardens and developed a clear agreement about the nature of their relationship. The rector tested his ideas with the senior warden on a regular basis. Both were helped by the arrangement because the rector could more effectively package his visionary agenda and the warden could see the necessity for changes in the congregation's life and direction. This was not an easy arrangement for either because they would often disagree, but their commitment to live in the tension created a model for this vestry and produced effective leadership decisions.

Relatedness

Definition

The relatedness scale measures the way members of an organization work together, especially whether their work is done cooperatively or independently.

At one pole we have *collegial* operation, which emphasizes cooperative efforts within the congregation as a whole to do the work of ministry. Most congregations tend to operate at the cooperative end of the scale—everything done in committee, very little by people acting alone or independently. This kind of an environment encourages collaboration. Harmony and peaceful relationship are the keys.

At the other end of the spectrum, the focus is on the *individual.* Premium is placed on individual initiative, on people working independently from one another. Individuals or small groups are freed to pursue their own interests and calling. There is not a lot of checking in. At this end of the scale, the organization is much more likely to encourage the free expression of ideas, to encourage difference, to allow or help people distance themselves from others in the group. People may be encouraged to be competitive, to stand out, to do their work without needing to report to anyone else.

Excesses at the Collegial End of the Scale

When the organization moves into excess at the collegial end of the relatedness scale, everything (well, almost everything) is done in committees. Members of the group do not seem secure unless they are working with someone. Little is done by people working alone.

This kind of environment can be overly concerned about preserving relationships. If people go off and do their own thing, they might come up with different ideas about how to proceed or new perceptions of what is needed. This could lead to competition or hurt feelings, which the organization in excess at the collegial end of the scale will experience as anathema. This results in an enmeshed system, that is, a system where it is difficult for people to separate themselves from one another. What another person does is immediately noticed and responded to and the response is generally experienced as cooperative. The behaviors are complementary.

A certain kind of conflict may be suppressed in an excessively collegial system. This is not reactive conflict, where the parties are engaged in a well-understood and choreographed dance in which actions and reactions are predictable; we expect so-and-so to blow up, and when he does, the rest of us withdraw. That is not the kind of conflict we are talking about here. We are talking about competitive conflict that emerges from people thinking independently and coming up with different ideas. In a collegial system, this doesn't feel appropriate. Because people expect unity, they are unable or unwilling to state clearly what they need from others. Sometimes those willing to risk dissent are labeled as troublemakers.

In an organization stuck in excess at the cooperative end of the scale, changes come slowly because many need to be consulted and most need to agree before action can be taken.

An Episcopal church we worked with in the late eighties did everything in committees. No one would think of acting alone or making a decision without careful consultation. Conflict was suppressed. Agreement was all important. *Fellowship* was the key word in the congregation. This got people into trouble because it was very difficult to take action. When emergencies arose (or decisions on which nobody would care which way the organization chose to go), they were stuck. They were not given permission to act.

When a change was to be made, *everybody* needed to be consulted. So many opinions were heard, with little consensus, that folks did not know what to choose. Consequently little work got done; and when conflict arose, they had no means with which to deal with it.

Excesses at the Individual End of the Scale

Of course, an organization can be in excess at the individual end of the scale as well. In this case turf becomes all important—what's mine, what's yours, and who gets control over what. Instead of responding to the fear of individual overcontrol by putting many in charge, the system in excess at the individual end of the scale tries to keep order by keeping the various parties or constituencies separate.

In this situation the relational "glue" is weakened and a more disengaged system develops. Patience and stamina to work collaborative decisions is limited. Indeed, patience sometimes "feels wrong." By "giving in" to the group, one loses his valued individuality, her valued creativity. Sometimes subgroups develop into antagonistic tribes that engage in power struggles. This can lead to open conflict, which becomes a congregational pastime.

In a downtown Episcopal church in a large metropolitan area the vestry met one hour each month. They were proud of the fact that they could get the work done so quickly. This was possible because the vestry would never dream of overriding a decision made by another individual or group. The junior warden took care of the building (never asking for help from a committee). The senior warden oversaw the budget (with no finance committee). The pastor did the program. Any existing committees did not meet and had nothing to report. When the rector or one of the wardens (or the church) had a problem, the vestry would hear about it—if it needed to know. Hearing about the problem, however, usually occurred after action has been taken on the problem, after it had been fixed or the contractor hired.

This congregation was having serious trouble developing any energy or excitement for their ongoing program, let alone new programs. The leaders had no one to lead, and the congregation began to wind down.

Living in the Tension

When the members of a congregation live in the tension between collegiality and individuation, they can take the initiative—but also explore its impact on others. In other words, the driving force of the tension is not naked self-interest but self-interests tempered by the interests of the larger group. Care is taken to identify individual needs and differences. At the same time, the work of individuals and small groups is tied to the overall purposes of the congregation. The work is reviewed in light of these larger purposes.

Where the tension is appropriate, collaborative decision making is encouraged but dissent and minority reports are expected. Leaders are encouraged to face differences around the issues of congregational life while taking care of one another in the midst of those differences.

Committees and work groups are large enough to get good samples of opinion but small enough to get the work done efficiently and meet the recognition needs of individuals. Committees are given authority and the board does not often redo or spend inordinate time checking over the work of a committee.

In the system where both cooperative and individuating forces are operative, people are valued as well as the work (the product). Work groups devote time to relationship building and spiritual development and to the accomplishment of task.

A Disciples of Christ congregation in Missouri is a good example of this kind of healthy tension. This church has a wide range of committee sizes, and many people are working on specific tasks outside of committees. The congregational board is fairly large (eighteen). Committees such as Christian Education that require work and commitment from people not on the committee are large enough to get samples of opinion but small enough to get work done (eight to twelve members). Many jobs in the church are done without the aid of a committee: treasurer, oversight of church maintenance, and head usher. All people in these positions are supervised and are expected to report regularly to the committee overseeing their work.

Lay Leadership

Definition

The language and concepts of the *lay leadership* scale are identical to those used for pastoral leadership. Like pastors, lay leaders will function somewhere between the needs of the moment and future desires—between the practicalities and the vision. Both poles of this lay-focused dimension are needed and both can contribute equally to effective leadership.

Managerial lay leaders place an emphasis on achieving doable goals. They want to know what the plan is and what part they play in that strategy.

Managerial leaders look for ways to organize resources toward a clear practical outcome. They are attuned to budgeting concerns but willing to realign budgets when a compelling data-based case can be made for the change.

Managerial lay leadership lends itself to the effective oversight of committees or other task groups. Managerial leaders will strive to ensure that the necessary resources are available to complete the work. They will track progress toward goals and work to solve problems that arise along the way. They are focused on practical results in the short-run and will organize others toward achieving those results. They will be attuned to the resource limitations (money and human energy) within their own department or area of ministry and strive to operate within those limitations. They will delegate responsibility to their committee members and follow up with those members where necessary.

Transformational lay leaders work to create change within their congregations. They have a larger vision for their congregation's future that involves new directions and new opportunities for ministry. They look farther into the future than their managerial counterparts and invite others toward that future. Transformational leaders enroll others in their vision, not by organizing people toward goals but by inspiring them to create change. They are willing to trust others to work out the details once the vision is caught.

This transformational dimension of lay leadership will introduce some risk taking into a congregation's life. It creates and articulates a compelling picture of the future that motivates people to push the boundaries of accepted methods and goals. Where congregations are experiencing strong environmental change that requires a shift in basic approaches to ministry, transformational leaders can lend courage. They can lead toward needed discontinuous change and help their colleagues to take leaps of faith.

Excesses at the Managerial End of the Scale

In lay leadership tension is more often lost toward the managerial end of the scale than toward the transformational end. Congregational systems tend to reward managerial behavior on the part of lay leaders. Even people who may exhibit transformational leadership outside the church may eventually devote their energies to the maintenance needs of the congregation and become watchdogs of budget and buildings. Sometimes this excess will develop in response to traumatic events such as a severe conflict that divided a congregation or the involuntary termination of a pastor. Lay leaders may pull back into a defensive retreat and avoid taking risks. In this retreat mode, "time horizons" are very short and a premium is placed upon practical agendas, harmony, and unity.

Lay leaders in this excess will be out of touch with the changes affecting their congregation or will minimize these changes by focusing on short-term events and immediate solutions. Managerial excesses prevent lay leaders from considering far-reaching strategies for congregational renewal or making significant shifts.

We have worked with a church board that demonstrated these excesses. The board took pride in maintaining a balanced budget, reducing organizational risks, and keeping track of time and property. They spent most of their time at board meetings discussing what the pastor got paid and whether or not to sell the parsonage—a large, fancy house they could not afford to keep up.

This board guided the congregation though a long-range planning process. The planning was well-organized and concluded in a timely fashion. There were five priorities:

— send out a list of officers and phone numbers to the members.
— ask ushers to guide worshippers to their seats after the service has started.
— repaint the loading-zone curbs in front of the church.
— repair the sign in front of the church.
— engage a company to produce a pictorial directory.

Excesses at the Transformational End of the Scale

When tension is lost at the transformational end of the scale, lay leaders fail to put structure around their change efforts. These excesses bring complaints from parishioners about a lack of responsible management or a lack of good stewardship of the congregation's resources. Transformational leaders in excess will launch new programs without having the funds in place to support them. Risk-taking endeavors not grounded in good management lead to a loss of trust in leaders.

Transformational excesses also create a values gap between lay leaders and parishioners. Too much change, too many new programs, leave parishioners with the impression that what was done in the past is no longer valued. In time, parishioners themselves feel devalued and wonder if their understanding of the church's purpose is still valid.

Multiple change efforts that are not grounded in the organizational life of the congregation produce chaos. Leaders and members in general burn out as they jump from one project to the next. People are not supported adequately in their efforts to do ministry and cannot achieve the expected results. New participants have to be recruited constantly to replace those leaving out of discouragement or fatigue.

While these excesses are found less often among lay leaders, we have worked with congregations where transformational leadership was overdone. In one case, a new church development—focused entirely on evangelism and winning souls for Christ—met in different locations around town. The pastor and lay leaders exhorted the other members to get out into the community and call on people. (No training was provided for this.)

People were excited about their new faith community together but had no time or energy for maintaining their institutions or taking care of the members. It was not clear where the next church service would be or when Bible study groups would meet or who would lead them. A core group of lay board members continued to put forth their vision about the congregation's future, but the congregation was unable to grow.

Living in the Tension

When both poles of this dimension are active, lay leaders put forth a clear vision for the congregation's future and then manage that vision into reality. Leadership is recruited, not simply to fill slots, but to match individual gifts with opportunities to lead. Lay leaders are expected to initiate change efforts (as opposed to leaving initiative with the pastor). Both managerial and transformational voices are valued in board meetings and conflict between the voices is expected and sometimes encouraged.

We have worked with a congregation that illustrates this tension. The lay leadership recently went through a long-range planning process. They looked into the future and realized that their neighborhood soon would draw fewer young families because property values had increased so dramatically. So the church decided to relocate in a newer, less expensive suburban area.

This congregation regularly faces these kinds of questions. Lay leaders are nurtured to challenge old patterns. This same group of lay leaders realized that many members wanted help with their spiritual growth. Instead of looking to more and better adult classes, the congregation decided to hire a theologian-in-residence (a year at a time) who would sit in on board and committee meetings and function as a teacher, counselor, preacher, and retreat leader.

These ministries (the new building and the theologian-in-residence) cost money that the church did not have at the time. Yet they had carefully thought out their belief—that by taking these actions they would generate more resources (which they did and then some).

Learning

Definition

The *learning* scale measures a congregation's orientation toward the past or the future as it experiments with improving its life and ministry.

An organization at the *maximizing* end of the scale has its attention fixed on the past. It asks itself, "From what have our successes come in the past? What are our strengths? Where do we have the most resources?" With this viewpoint a congregation builds on its strengths.

At the other end of this scale, *metamizing* looks beyond the congregation's current strengths to develop something new. (This does not necessarily mean giving up using one's strength—though it could; it is more likely to mean experimenting with the development of untried programs or methods of approaching ministry.) These new competencies could be discontinuous with the past. For example, the congregation may not have had much of a strength with music, but it might want to explore changing and developing the Sunday morning worship.

Excesses at the Maximizing End of the Scale

We said this before, but it bears repeating: In the successes of an organization are the seeds of failure. When past successes become present ruts or when old successful patterns no longer meet the needs of the present constituencies, pushing those "old buttons" will lead the organization further from accomplishment.

In a church focusing on past success, people with new ideas or approaches become discouraged. The leadership of the system doesn't pay attention, or gets annoyed, or puts up obstacle after obstacle, demotivating those with enthusiasm.

But incremental improvements in existing programs and processes lull congregational leaders into believing that they are effectively responding to the needs of the membership and the community. They tend to discount the fact of numerical decline while pointing to their programmatic success.

A Presbyterian church in the Northwest used the Callahan planning process, which encourages organizations to build on their strengths. This drove them toward excess by identifying adult education, social ministry, and worship as strengths and asking how each could be improved. For example, the church concluded that its social ministry was too much a cafeteria-style operation with money and efforts scattered in different directions. It would improve the strategy by focusing energies on a few key ministries. But this led to small interest groups pushing harder and harder for their particular concerns and to other people disengaging because they were not interested in those ministries but found no other place to plug in to serve.

This church does the same things over and over again, driving their habits—and the church—into the ground. The excess leads to an odd paradox in which successes could be celebrated as old strengths are improved, but the overall impact on the life and health of this declining congregation is minimal.

In some ways this excess enables congregational leadership to live inside of its own reality, which produces ongoing or even increasing confidence in the established directions and programs, while becoming more and more blind to the congregation's inability to respond to changing circumstances and changing opportunities. In the absence of a constructive tension between the old success and new possibilities, the congregational learning system turns inward and creates a paralysis.

Excesses at the Metamizing End of the Scale

Congregations in excess at the metamizing end of the learning scale are vulnerable to current trends and fads. Instead of doing anything well, they run about doing the latest thing. Leaders may neglect or abandon basic strengths of the congregation and lose those who were nourished by those strengths.

In these congregations those who initiate change do so discontinuously, abruptly. When this happens, the leadership becomes isolated from the rest of the congregation, or the congregation mightily resists through fighting or noncooperation the "creative" experiments in ministry (whether they are abruptly initiated or not). Too much experimentation fragments the congregation, increases discord, and causes the tradition-bound members to entrench.

In this excess, a church is usually not unified at either end of the scale. The congregation may be polarized in its approach to change. Congregations that are somewhat unified in their excess at the metamizing end of the scale run the risk of losing their identity as a result of the many changes. They may be changing so much, and so often, that they lose their core, their commitment, their sense of who they are.

There is another obvious difficulty with metamizing in the excess: Experimental programs can be initiated without adequate resources. People with great program ideas sometimes don't take the time to think through how much it will cost, how many volunteer hours the work will take, what impact the programs will have on other programs. Perhaps you have known of a congregation that had a pretty good youth program—until it hired a minister of music for teenagers who functioned as the Pied Piper, drawing teenagers into the youth choirs and out of the youth fellowship group.

We know a congregation in Arizona where the congregation regularly moves from one part of town to another (renting hotel banquet rooms). What's more, every Sunday the service of worship is "surprise": new speakers, new orders of worship, new music, new ways of using audio-visuals (drama, dance, overheads, films, etc.). The congregation does attract quite a few new people, but it seems to loose as many as it brings in. Newcomers tend not to stay more than four to six months.

Living in the Tension

Living in the tension means that the leaders of the church know the congregation's current distinctive competencies and help it celebrate these gifts from God. They are slow to abandon successful ministries but regularly experiment with new opportunities for ministry. Maximizing and metamizing voices are kept in dialogue.

The two ends of the spectrum are kept in tension by making sure that new projects are connected to a long-range plan. The church leadership is attentive to the need to experiment and to build on the strengths of the organization.

In such a congregation leaders recognize that developing a new congregational strength takes time. They cultivate new projects, providing adequate timelines for people to participate in the decision making, get used to new ideas and projects, and develop them incrementally. When programs are initiated, evaluation procedures are established to avoid premature abandonment of an experiment or to modify as needed.

A successful evangelical congregation downtown in a large mid-western city has a program of cell groups that meet weekly. Some of these groups choose to meet year after year and are not open to new members. Other groups are formed two times a year at a church fair where people who do not belong to a cell are invited to join groups looking for new members or new groups. Church leaders propose new study groups as interest or need arises. Some of these are short-term groups; some are long-term.

You can see that this congregation does not keep doing the same thing—though there are people who do.

Conclusion

By now you should have a grasp of the dimensions highlighted here and in the Congregational Systems Inventory. These congregational dimensions do not exhaust all possibilities but are those we feel most accessible to church leadership.

S. L. and G. P.

CHAPTER V

Analyzing the Profile

Interpreting Scores

The Congregational Systems Inventory is designed to be used with a leadership group so that multiple perspectives can contribute to a composite church profile. For reasons mentioned earlier, we believe that relatively few people will have a thorough overview of the organizational aspects of a congregation's life. Interpretive material in this chapter assumes that the results of at least twelve individual profiles have been combined to create a composite profile. (A rule of thumb would be to base the number of profiles on the Rothauge categorization[1] of church size: Family-sized Church, twelve to fifteen profiles; Pastoral-sized Church, fifteen to twenty profiles; Program-sized Church, twenty to thirty-five profiles; Corporate-sized Church, thirty to forty-five profiles.)

Individual inventory responses collated on the score sheet score between 0 and 10 for each dimension. When a number of individual scores are placed on the continuum for each dimension, the groupings will indicate the degree of relative tension in the congregation. Because you will be working with multiple scores, you will want to show the range of scores, note where scores tend to cluster, and perhaps produce a mean score for each dimension.

A pattern of scores plotted toward the center of the continuum (4 to 6) indicate an approximation of optimum tension between contending opposites. In example 5-1 note that the scores are clustered toward the center of the continuum. In this case the congregation maintained a good tension between its ability to concentrate authority in groups and individuals and to disperse authority so that people could adequately participate in and influence decision making.

Example 5-1:
Authority

Concentrated   Dispersed

	1	3	6	6	8	3	1			
0	1	2	3	4	5	6	7	8	9	10

A pattern of scores plotted toward one end (0 to 3) or the other (7 to 10) would indicate a loss of tension and a dominance by one excess or the risk of excessive reliance on that tendency. Such a pattern may suggest needed changes for a congregation and will usually identify potential stumbling blocks to change. Example 5-2, taken from a Program-sized Church locked in a factional dispute over its pastor's tenure, shows a clear excess.

Example 5-2:
Strategy

Planned   Spontaneous

				2		4	2	8	10	2
0	1	2	3	4	5	6	7	8	9	10

In this example, the range of scores, the cluster, and the mean (computed by multiplying the number of responses by their value and then dividing the totaled values by the total number of responses) all show this church to be in excess at the spontaneous end of the scale. This congregation has no plan, is confused about its direction, and allows individual criteria to be brought to bear on a pastor's performance.

Reading the Overall Profile

The composite result on each scale can offer valuable information about your congregation. The board and staff of the congregation in example 5-2 recognized that proceeding with change efforts would be unproductive until they developed a long-range plan.

Taken individually, each dimension will offer important clues about the nature of a congregation's system. Comparing each of the seven scales to the others can provide a comprehensive view of the congregation as an organizational system. This systemic view will suggest more focused strategies and priorities for the congregational leadership.

Example 5-3 shows the overall profile of a Program-sized suburban Lutheran church that sought consultation before developing a long-range plan. A quick scan of this profile shows a loss of tension on six of the seven scales.

Example 5-3:

Strategy

Planned   Spontaneous

						1	6	6	2	
0	1	2	3	4	5	6	7	8	9	10

Authority

Concentrated   Dispersed

	4	2	1	2	2	2	2			
0	1	2	3	4	5	6	7	8	9	10

Process

Mandatory   Discretionary

0	1	2	3	4	5	6	7	8	9	10
				2	1	3	2	5	2	

Pastoral Leadership

Managerial   Transformational

0	1	2	3	4	5	6	7	8	9	10
1	1		1	1	2	1	3	2	2	1

Relatedness

Collegial   Individual

0	1	2	3	4	5	6	7	8	9	10
		2	1	2	3	2	2	1	2	

Lay Leadership

Managerial   Transformational

0	1	2	3	4	5	6	7	8	9	10
2	6	3	1	2	1					

Learning

Maximize   Metamize

0	1	2	3	4	5	6	7	8	9	10
2	5	2		2	2	2				

Spontaneous strategy: The congregation has no clearly defined vision or direction.

Concentrated authority: Smaller groups (and in this case the pastor) have an undue amount of influence, potentially blocking efforts to develop a participatory approach to long-range planning or decision making in general.

Discretionary process: Their organizational and structural life is underdeveloped, especially for their size. People do not have enough structure to do their jobs, communication among groups is haphazard, and no process exists for dealing with contention. This excess further drives the concentration of authority.

Transformational pastor: The pastor is trying to introduce needed changes but is not providing the structure to contain the change. He loses touch with his parishioners, doesn't follow through with ideas, and conveys his frustration about the lack of vision, lazy lay leaders, and a general lack of receptivity to his leadership.

Managerial lay leaders: Council members are committed, responsible leaders who act more and more as the "brakes" to the pastor's "accelerator." They are worn out from their efforts to keep the program and administrative functions going. They are also frustrated and perplexed by their inability to implement plans and ideas and to deal with the emerging conflicts in this congregation.

Maximized learning: The congregation stays with past successes and does not venture into new endeavors, programs, or organizational strategies. Strongly tradition-bound, they will work to build the future on the past.

It is not uncommon to see this combination of excesses from opposite sides of the continua, some pointing toward overcontrol and some toward chaos. The result is a marriage of rigidity and disorganization. Concentrated authority and maximized learning combine to keep this congregation in the past, while managerial lay leaders try to hold back the effects of change and internal strife. Spontaneous strategy and discretionary process combine to foster disorganization and the lack of a collective effort to address the issues at hand.

A transformational pastor working with managerial lay leaders in this case created an impasse partly because of the interpersonal dynamics among them and the pastor's autocratic philosophy of leadership. Yet the mix of transformational pastor and managerial lay leaders can become a plus for a congregation if they can enter an enduring dialogue that reclaims good leadership tension. As a team they have the requisite perspectives to lead this congregation into a new era. But using those perspectives to full advantage requires a willingness to talk candidly and to treat one another with respect.

This congregation also has a healthy tension on the relatedness scale. People value their relationships and enjoy the many ways they team up to work together. They also can speak their minds to one another and tolerate a diverse spectrum of opinions and beliefs. The flexibility created by this tension can become an important asset during a change process. Approaches to long-range planning that suppress differences are more likely to fail.

Without significant efforts to regain tension in at least three of the seven scales, a long-range plan for this church will be blocked by interest groups, will likely underestimate the extent of change necessary for a healthy future, and eventually will be shelved and forgotten. While this congregation may be tempted first to address the strategy dimension, they will initially need to attend to their structural life (process) and build a working relationship between the pastor and the council. Participatory approaches to planning, involving groups that have garnered authority over the years, should be designed. A full discussion of change strategies for each scale follows in chapters 6 through 12.

Trouble-Shooting Guide

Rejecting Inventory Items

The forced choices in the CSI will cause some participants to check neither option or both options in a given item. Before completing the inventory, participants can be reminded that some of the choices will be difficult and only distantly approximate their actual personal view of the congregation. Encourage them to make a choice for every item. The instrument will not choose for them. If participants check neither option or both options in a given item, it will invalidate their score on the inventory.

Scattered Range of Scores

In some profile scales, scores will be scattered oddly across the continuum without an identifiable cluster. (See diagram 1.) This may occur
because some participants are relatively new to leadership roles or to the
church and cannot adequately assess a particular dimension. Or it may
occur when a congregation is severely conflicted as some participants
will take extreme positions relative to some dimensions, contributing
very high (9, 10) or very low (0, 1) scores.

Diagram 1

Strategy

Planned   Spontaneous

1	2	1	3	1	2	1	3	0	2	1
0	1	2	3	4	5	6	7	8	9	10

A scattering of scores is an opportunity to invite dialogue. You may
group those with very low scores together with those with high scores
and ask them to share their perspectives about that particular dimension.
Be aware that a scattering may also indicate that the data is not trustworthy. On that particular scale you may not be able to draw any conclusion
at all.

Scoring Discrepancies between Clergy and Laity

In our experience, clergy scores on the CSI tend to correspond to the
composite score created by the lay leaders. The one exception has been
in relation to the pastoral leadership scale. Here clergy scores tend to be
more extreme (in either direction) than those of their lay leaders. Where
this occurs we suggest that you encourage a dialogue to explore the
discrepancy. Sometimes pastors respond to the leadership questions in
terms of their intent and their values rather than their actual behavior.

Congregations at Higher Levels of Conflict

We do not recommend administering the CSI to groups engaged in significant conflict.[2] People will (a) tend to use the inventory as a weapon by giving extreme, all-or-nothing responses; or (b) not complete the inventory at all; or (c) partially complete the inventory and complain that the choices are impossible. As groups move to lower levels of conflict, the inventory can provide useful guidance for future steps as well as clues about the sources of the difficulty they have been experiencing.

People with Extreme Scores

Some people may score extremely high or low on most or all of the scales. This may occur because that person has a philosophical or theological perspective that departs dramatically from the membership as a whole or because the person is in conflict with the leadership of the congregation. Or this person may be thinking of a particular part of the organization, or a particular time in its life. We have sometimes found it helpful to invite comments from those whose scores place them well outside the group range. The benefits of this conversation need to be balanced against the reality being described by the overall profile results.

Clustered Scores at Both Ends of the Scale

Diagram 2 is an example of a split cluster.

Diagram 2

Learning

Maximize										Metamize
0	1	7	4	1	2	2	5	6	0	0
0	1	2	3	4	5	6	7	8	9	10

This phenomenon presents another opportunity for group dialogue. It may reflect generational or theological differences or more severe conflict within the group. This example was taken from a congregation that had many new members and a corresponding change in the leadership circle. The longer-tenured members rated the congregation toward the metamizing end of the scale. Typical comments from this group included, "We have too many new programs now"; "The pastor has focused too much on making changes"; and "We've lost sight of our basic strengths." The newer members rated the congregation toward the maximizing end and said, "We are slow to change around here"; "People want to keep doing the things that worked ten years ago!"

Split clusters may reflect a loss of tension if the two perspectives are not able to work together, face the differences, and take care of their relationships as they make decisions. The two groups will retreat to their poles and act out the excesses in ways that exacerbate conflict and block creative decision making.

G. P.

CHAPTER VI

Strategies
for Reclaiming Tension

This chapter is about change but not "change for the sake of change." If that were the topic at hand, as authors we would be in excess on a continuum between stability and change or adaptation. This chapter is addressed to organizations in excess at either end of a CSI polarity. *Change* as described here is about moving out of the excess toward a moderation and flexibility—toward keeping an appropriate tension alive.

The most powerful factors affecting organizational change are outside the control of the leadership or the organization. Most organizational changes are brought about in response to surprisingly powerful assaults from sources thought to be under control or from ambushes that catch leadership completely off guard. When organizations change, they are usually adapting to something that has happened to them rather than consciously deciding that such-and-such would be good to do.

Adapting to outside forces is absolutely necessary for survival. The organization that is able to respond appropriately to outside (or inside) forces—adapting, accommodating, adjusting—is most likely to survive. If the organization is not adapting (for survival purposes) to changing conditions, it will be unable to initiate or carry out transformational activities (transforming either the organization itself or realities beyond it).

The two most powerful and constant factors affecting any organization are (1) demographic or environmental forces and (2) developmental forces. These two realities will always be more powerful than intentional changes that individuals and committees conceive to enhance (or diminish) the quality of life or the effectiveness of a congregation.

It is our thesis that congregations that can respond appropriately to demographic and developmental forces have the best chance of moving beyond survival (adaptive) responses to making a difference. We realize that "making a difference" is a hackneyed way to talk about change, but we want to emphasize two dimensions to change: (1) adapting to changes brought about by environmental or developmental forces (this is not necessarily accomplishing anything more than staying alive), and (2) becoming conscious of possibilities of new ways of acting and doing.

Congregations provide a wonderful opportunity for people to practice the arts of managing the tensions of this world and engage in re-demptive change. Sometimes we would like to skip the tensions-of-this-world part and get on with the redemptive-change component. But many endeavors to make a difference misfire because they are not grounded in what is actually going on in the environment or the organization.

Several general change strategies are critical to the change pro-cess—to keeping appropriate tension alive. These general strategies are (1) capitalizing on the environmental forces; (2) becoming conscious of the tacit contracts that have been established among the parties in the system; (3) keeping contention alive; (4) recontracting; (5) disturbing the equilibrium; (6) and training. They underlie the particular strategies we will be discussing in chapters VII through XII. Let's look at these six general strategies.

Capitalizing on the Environmental and Developmental Forces

Many environmental forces from outside the life of a congregation are affecting its growth and decline: location (for example, we know that most congregations take on the look, demographically, of their surround-ing neighborhoods); financial health (for example, when people are out of work or retired, they generally give less than when they have regular incomes); the interests of the members (for example, of late people have been more interested in spiritual growth than previously); and the ways people relate to one another (for example, recently the church has seen significant change in the use of gender-inclusive language in worship, hymnals, and everyday parlance).

Developmental tasks are another powerful force influencing the life of a congregation. Brand new congregations (church starts), if they are growing, go through recognizable evolutions that force change on the system. When the congregation is brand new, it is probably structured around the personality of one or two leaders and/or the pastor. Quite likely its meetings are not every week and often not on Sundays. As the church grows, it finds a regular place to worship and it develops programs. These developmental tasks seem to be built into the life of a new and growing congregation.

Congregations face another developmental task when a pastor leaves the congregation and the pulpit is left vacant. This normal and natural occurrence requires the organization to find different leadership for the day-to-day work. Laity often take on more responsibility and authority. Some programs get dropped. Many members become more active and interested in what the board is up to during the interim between tenured clergy.

When confronted with changing developmental tasks or environmental forces, the church is frequently thrown out of its homeostasis. The natural response of the congregation is to try to pull the church back into the old patterns and ways of doing things. Even this reaction is a movement of the organization, a response that shows that the organization is not frozen but has the capacity at least to attempt to regain its balance if not change its patterns.

As the system shifts, energy is released, members see themselves and others in new ways, and nonconscious contracts or patterns become conscious. This is why interim ministry can be a boon to congregational life. While the congregation is in the flux of change from clergy to lay leadership and back to clergy leadership again, it is in an unfrozen state where changes can be effected more easily than when the congregation has settled into familiar patterns.

Becoming Conscious

Of course, there is no always-right way to approach change. As we have said, sometimes the organization is too ensconced at the chaotic end of things, sometimes at the constrictive end of things. But the first test is always to identify what is going on. Using the CSI, of course, is one useful way to assess the extent to which the organization is stuck at either end of the scale.

There are other ways to appraise what is happening. Simple observation can be very helpful. If there is more than one observer, note that one person's "tight" can be another person's "loose." You'll want to get several opinions before deciding, *Yes, indeed, we've got too much concentrated authority around here.*

Most students of organizational theory believe that insiders (members, staff) may not be able to see the contracts they have made with one another to keep the organization at the loose or tight end of the scale. These contracts are often nonconscious, and part of this nonconscious contracting may include the pattern of denying or discounting certain behavior or practices that are affecting it. Considering this, you might invite trustworthy outsiders into the organization to help the parties assess what is happening. Newcomers are more likely to see what is happening than old timers. Somehow we get used to the way things are, and we believe the status quo is okay.

In my (Leas) town there's a small supermarket that had been deteriorating for years. Few in town noticed it. We all had gotten used to the crowded aisles, the dingy conditions, the not-so-fresh vegetables. That is the way it was at the Super. We remember being asked in a survey to comment on the market. "Oh, it's fine," we said. "It's close. They've got what you need in an emergency. We know where to find things. We don't need 'fancy' here in our little town."

But fewer customers were shopping there, and the management was wise enough, or hurting enough, to fix the place up. The vegetables improved; the aisles were widened; new equipment was installed including shelves, lighting, even a laser scanner at the checkout. It's our understanding that business is picking up. But did that mean there was a cry of joy in town? Not by many regulars. "You can't find anything in here anymore," we heard one man say. "You sure are getting uppity around here," opined another to an innocent $4.15 per hour cashier.

To keep up with the times, or should we say the market, the store had to be able to move out of its traditional stance, its satisfaction with "good enough." It had to notice that there was a problem and respond. This meant some hardship for everyone. The owners had to get financing. The buyers were inconvenienced while the changes were made and couldn't find what they were looking for after the changes had been made. The competition in the next town noticed a drop in sales, and the bread-truck driver got chewed out for not being careful with his bread cart on the new floors. Everyone felt some tension because of the changes.

For a congregation (or a store) to embrace (and hold on to) the tension that comes from change, folks have to know that it is worth it, that tension is normal; indeed, it is a sign of caring about the organization. If we lose perspective on (1) what is needed (the gain) and (2) the pain (the normal response), then the homeostatic forces will hold the congregation back from real change.

Keeping Contention Alive

This principle of organizational change seems at first to go against one's intuition. We are tempted to minimize the impact of the disparity by attempting to keep the peace, to move too rapidly to solve the problem before the problem is clearly defined (or when it is erroneously defined), or to focus on symptoms, such as another's personality or behavior, and lose sight of other, perhaps more fundamental, issues.

This principle of keeping the tension alive plays an important role in getting to the root of the homeostatic excesses. Tension is the pushing of one pole against the other, one party's needs against the others. How *tension* of change is handled and managed can make the difference between being successful and effective or being marginally successful and ineffective in managing change. Tension, understood and managed correctly, can energize an organization or help bind it together, especially if we avoid: (1) using force to dictate a solution; (2) withdrawing or avoiding the tension; and (3) giving up one's own needs to end the tension.

These three ways of dealing with tension are often counterproductive in that they do not help the parties get all the information or see one another's viewpoints. They do not hold people in problem-solving activities until they find solutions that meet a broad range of interests and needs.

Recontracting

This is probably the most common way of bringing about change in organizations. Recontracting assumes that we can name the contract that we now have. Frequently the recontracting is around formal or informal roles: How much authority should the pastor have over the worship

service? What responsibilities should the treasurer have? Should we
continue to ask Mary Louise to use her van for transporting the high-
school group?

Tacit contracts are much more difficult to deal with because (1)
people don't even know they have these agreements, and (2) these patterns are generally ingrained and difficult to change. Nonetheless, to the
extent that we can become conscious of the contracts that have been
made, we can, through informal and formal recontracting, attempt to
instill in our consciousness a new understanding of how we are going to
deal with one another. Of course our nonconscious selves may still try to
sabotage the conscious agreements we are making. But there is no
chance of changing the nonconscious agreements until we have some
understanding and some kind of commitment by all (or at least most of)
the parties that they want to interact in different ways.[1]

Disturbing the Equilibrium

Inevitably, any conscious or nonconscious change effort will disturb the
equilibrium of an organization, and the homeostatic forces will try to
keep things the "way they were." One can attempt to cause organizational change by recontracting; in this case the parties affected by the
change are aware that there is a problem (or that someone thinks there is
a problem). Or one can attempt to cause change by taking initiatives in
unusual ways or by responding atypically to others' initiatives. In this
section, "disturbing the equilibrium" means taking initiatives or responding to others' initiatives in ways that do not fit expectations for the
normal patterns of behavior in the organization.

Disturbing the equilibrium is often a serious problem for the organization. If, because of depression, the pastor is withdrawing from his
usual contact with parishioners (informal time spent with members at
coffee Sunday morning, check-in calls with key leaders of the church,
agenda-setting meetings with chairs of committees), the organization is
apt to respond by trying to restore the system to the old standards of
communication. These responses might include moving toward the
pastor in positive and assertive ways ("What's going on with you? I
haven't heard from you as often as I used to.") or in aggressive and
antagonistic ways ("The pastor doesn't care about the members of this

church; he certainly is self-centered.") The point is that action in a
system gets response (reaction). Both the actor and the responder have
choices about the kinds of responses they are going to make. When the
action or response is out of the normal pattern, the equilibrium is dis-
turbed.

One can consciously (or nonconsciously) go about disturbing the
equilibrium in many ways. Much of what follows in chapters VII
through XII describes ways to disturb the equilibrium. Adding newcomers to committees disturbs the equilibrium of the system in that neo-
phytes ask the "wrong" questions and respond "peculiarly" to others'
initiatives. Reducing or enlarging the size of committees impacts a
system in ways that elicit responses that move the system.

Disturbing the equilibrium is not always a matter of fiddling with
the size or constituency of a committee or group. One can also disturb
the equilibrium by acting in new, unexpected ways. For example, a
pastor who has always made follow-up calls to be sure that responsibilities are fulfilled before committee meetings may deliberately stop re-
minding people of what they had promised to do and stop helping them
do their work. But with this tactic the organization can respond in a
variety of ways; none is guaranteed: It can get mad at the pastor for
dereliction of duty; it can move toward the pastor, asking if something is
wrong; it can move another person(s) into the "reminder" role; or each
person can take more personal responsibility for his or her part in the
organization. Disturbing the equilibrium without also inviting people
into a recontracting discussion can lead to unpredictable effects.

Sometimes people disturb the equilibrium and interrupt the interaction patterns not by taking initiative differently but by responding in
unconventional ways. For example, in one congregation the members
had developed a pattern of chewing each other out in very short, very
harsh speeches made at board and committee meetings. The usual response had been for the person being attacked to become silent, for observers to become silent, for the subject to be changed by a third party,
and then for the issue or the behavior not to be referred to again (in a
meeting). There seemed to be only one way of dealing with difficulty:
a short angry outburst followed by sullen withdrawal by everyone in the
meeting. This put those willing to engage in aggressive behavior in a
powerful position if they wanted to stop something in the church. It
didn't help them start anything.

A newcomer to the deacons who didn't know the rules, or had decided not to play by them, responded to an attack in a meeting by saying, "I am surprised that you have a problem with my position. I think I have some good ideas about this subject, and I would like to know what your ideas about it are." At another meeting he responded to an attack on another member by saying, "Your response to Jim feels more like an attack on Jim's person than an argument related to the subject he has raised. I would like to hear more about your understanding of the subject."

These kinds of responses at first shocked the group. They had no idea how to respond to this kind of behavior. Of course, at first they changed the subject. It felt as if his responses were attacks too. After a while two things happened—personal attacks lessened, and others began to respond to attacks by inviting further discussion rather than withdrawing.

This is an example of someone disturbing the equilibrium where the story turned out well for the deacons. But it could have turned out in other ways. The attacking behavior could have increased. To get the newcomer to conform to the old rules, the withdrawal could have become even more obvious and members could have felt even more powerless.

Training

Finally, training can be a general change strategy, facilitating intervention in systems locked in excess. People can be trained to learn new ways of responding to and recontracting with one another. It is obvious that training a few people in an entrenched system will make it difficult for people attempting to use new ways. The more who "get it," the more who agree that they want to try new ways of handling one another, the greater the probability of bringing about systemic change.

As church consultants we hear people say, "That was helpful. I learned a lot. Too bad the people who really needed it were not here." This comment reveals the powerlessness a person feels believing that he or she cannot change, or that the organization cannot do better until "they" get fixed—and the fixing should be done by the consultant.

Training can be helpful to the system—as participants understand themselves as the disturbers of the equilibrium, continually inviting others to act and respond in ways that challenge or interrupt the old patterns of behavior. But if the members of the system believe that each person must figure out for himself or herself what must be done before it will get better, then all are victims of a one-by-one, nearly impossible individuated process.

When it comes to training, learning new skills is a slow process. It does not happen overnight. One does not learn skills by hearing about them or watching someone else do them. (This, of course, can be helpful, even necessary, but it is usually not sufficient.) When you learn to play tennis, you find that becoming successful requires not only intellectually understanding what the moves should be, but it also requires you to learn to connect that intellectual understanding with your body movements. Understanding and performing are two different realities. Then also, your ability to perform depends a great deal on what you are up against. You may have a great forehand when your opponent hits the ball to you slowly; you can easily position yourself for the shot. But if the ball comes fast, at an inconvenient spot, your return may leave something to be desired.

Training in organizational management, planning, conflict management, healthy living in tension, and so on, partakes of these same tennis realities. One needs both the intellectual understanding and the practice to be accomplished at the skill.

S. L.

CHAPTER VII

Moving Out of Excess: The Strategy Scale

In chapters VII through XII we will discuss more specific strategies that might be used to move out of particular excesses at either end of the scale. Each of the specific strategies addressed is an example that would fit under the six general strategies described in chapter VI: capitalizing on the environmental forces, becoming conscious of the tacit contracts that have been established between the parties in the system, keeping contention alive, recontracting, disturbing the equilibrium, and training. We'll look at each CSI scale, starting with *strategy*.

Again, strategy has to do with planning, with the way an organization thinks ahead. Sometimes the organization overplans (is in excess at the planned end of the scale); sometimes it underplans (is in excess at the spontaneous end of the scale).

The various change strategies we are proposing on the "strategy" scale give the reader ideas about ways to loosen or tighten the system with regard to planning. This list is not exhaustive; indeed, it is merely suggestive. We do hope that it will give you ideas about various ways you and/or your church board might think about changing the system so that it is more malleable, more pliable, less rigid, and better able to keep this polarity in tension.

Strategies to Move from Excess at the Planned End of the Scale

Take Longer and Involve More People in the Planning Process

A sure way to mess up a tight planning process is to get more people to present ideas. Some congregations (those that do any planning at all) believe that an annual board retreat—Friday night, Saturday morning and afternoon—is about enough planning for any church. Often this retreat includes ideas from a consultant, denominational executive, or pastor of a church across town. With the meals, the breaks, and the lecture by the noted authority, about two to three solid hours is left for planning. Often the board invites along spouses and key leaders from other parts of the church. This kind of retreat structure ensures that.

— The board is overwhelmed with many ideas, from paving the parking lot to providing more opportunities for spiritual growth in the adult education program.
— Hard issues are not confronted because the group does not have enough time with so many people in the discussion.
— The pastor and a few people (probably the executive committee) decide what the agenda will be for subsequent board meetings.
— The board ends up choosing things on which the largest number of people can agree.
— It is difficult in so short a time to convince people to take risks, to experiment with new ideas and new programs.

In other words, if you want to keep strategy in excess at the planned end of the scale, make sure that many people have a short time to discuss what they are about. To move toward the spontaneous end of the scale, get more ideas (from more people) and make it possible for them to find ways to articulate their vision seriously.

Take Lay Leaders through Creativity Training

The strategy dimension of a system can be loosened by inviting the
leaders to explore alternative scenarios about what the future might be
like. This kind of dreaming might help some break out of their focus on
a few select concerns to discover other needs and other ways the church
can respond.[1]

"What if the church were given a grant of $100,000? How would
we use it?" Here are some other "what if?" questions that might be used.

— What if we had a staff of four full-time professionals?
— What if we were able to move to a new location?
— What if all of our volunteers really did have one full day a
week to devote to ministry in this congregation?

Do Revisioning Exercises

Help people dream about what this church might become. You might
take the group on a guided imagery "magic carpet" tour of the church ten
years from now, noticing how the church will be different if your dreams
for the congregation were to come true. These dreams, while they can be
exciting and provocative, need time to germinate, and enough attention
(nourishment) to develop into ideas that can survive.

Revisioning requires:

— Safety—it is okay to think about different kinds of futures.
— Experimentation—new ideas need to be tried, tested, reshaped.
(A good way to keep the congregation in excess at the planned
end of the scale is to dream without experimentation. Think
ing up ideas forever and not trying any of them out keeps the
organization bound to the status quo.)
— Resources—volunteers, some space, and, perhaps, money to
try out the ideas. (If one's dreaming is to manifest itself in
action, there must be people acting on the dream. Acting on
the dream will probably mean changes in action by staff and
volunteers, changes in budget, and, often, change in the use of
the building.)

Move Authority to the Centers of Ministry

If initiative for finding new ideas for congregational life is put in the hands of the people primarily responsible for maintaining the organization, they are going to come up with maintenance-type ideas. If initiative for finding new ideas for congregational life is put in the hands of people who see their task as helping people grow—or become educated or provide good music or reach out to inactive members—these people will bring in ideas that challenge the congregation's needs for order, safety, security, constancy. If you keep the authority exclusively (or extensively) in the hands of those who seek to maintain the system, you reduce spontaneity.

As we said in an earlier chapter, authority can come from the right, given by the organization to people to make decisions for the larger group. Authority also comes from competence, ability, excitement, experience, and enthusiasm related to organizational tasks. If most of the authority is concentrated in those responsible for maintaining the safety and stability of the organization, if there is not a counterbalancing authority in the other parts of the organization's life, maintenance will overpower any tension that might be experienced from the pull of other authorities.

Get More Participation from the Grass Roots

One can go further down into the organization's system, not just to the boards and committees, but also to those who are involved in only the worship aspect of the congregation's life. Newcomers, people with new ideas, people with different experiences can loosen an organization substantially, especially if they are not partisans of the congregation's party line about what the church is supposed to do.

It is easy to maintain the excess at the planned end of the scale by involving everybody in short-term, make-the-list-too-long brainstorming sessions. Here what looks like movement toward spontaneity actually keeps the control in the hands of those who want to maintain the status quo.

This chapter is being written when Ross Perot, running for president of the United States, says he would take tough governmental decisions to the people. He would hold forums all over the country to discuss the issues, and then decisions would be made based on the will of the majority. While this kind of input clearly can do a lot to open the process, it can also become a means to support not experimenting, not responding differently, or not responding at all.

Provide Experiences for Lay Leaders to Interact with Their Environment

This is, perhaps, one of the most powerful ways to open new vistas to members of the congregation. New environments, new contacts, new relationships can change the way people see their world. It can change their priorities. As any Gestalt therapist would tell you, as one's focus changes, one's understanding of the world changes. Look at the figure below. Do you see two Xs, two Vs, or an M and a W?

If you saw two Xs, having someone who sees two Vs or eight Vs can break you out of old patterns. Having people point out different ways of seeing things can give us new insights.

Providing experiences for lay leaders to interact with their environment can take a variety of forms. One can bring in the environment. Invite speakers, community leaders, consultants, organizers, and experts on certain aspects of community life to engage in dialogue with church members or planning committees.

One can send out members to agencies, action groups, associations, etc. This process involves making appointments with people, telling them why you are coming, what you would like to learn, and how long you think the discussion will take. Or the parishioners can put themselves into the life of the community, talking with people informally about their experience, their needs, their interests, their hopes.[2]

Put New Congregational Members on Boards

Folks who have been with one another for a period of time can contaminate one another's dreams. We begin to develop a belief system about what is possible, what has failed in the past (and what we believe certainly will fail in the future). Newcomers come with a beginner's mind that helps them see things that the rest believe don't exist or are not possible. They can bring an enthusiasm and vigor that the rest have lost. People with new visions help some of us break out of old visions; they help us dream new dreams.

Look for People with Different Values, Ideas to Put on Boards

Congregations can screen out those who are different by choosing to elect or appoint to boards those who get along, who see things the same way as the others in leadership. Again, new ideas, less "tacit screening," can open up the planning process to spontaneity.

Encourage People to "Let the Holy Spirit Lead Us"

Prayer, meditation, and Bible study can be powerful influencers of a congregation's life. Making sure that we structure time for listening rather than telling or complaining can remind church members that their help is in the Lord, not just in their own experience. Slowing down the planning process to wait on the Lord can help move a group beyond being satisfied with what has worked in the past or is manageable based on their limited experience.

Summary

Notice this section focuses on dreaming, envisioning, and discernment. There is a need for congregations to do more than just dream; they also need to find ways to experiment. It is not enough to move and operate out of the spontaneous end of the strategy scale. Dreaming dreams but not attempting to carry them out is ultimately remaining stuck at the planned end of the strategy scale. Without experimentation, planning maintains the strategy status quo—because the response to new opportunities doesn't change. The trick here is to try new things, do things differently. Occasional talk of how things might be different doesn't effect change.

As a congregation becomes more spontaneous, its regular, consistent, life-shaping patterns function less rigidly. How rigid are our expectations about what we should be doing? How much flexibility do we have with regard to responding differently to financial needs, worship, money-raising activities, and so on?

Certain activities often associated with planning can actually loosen the rigidly planned system; brainstorming, envisioning, and prayer can help a group explore ideas about what to do and how to do it. One gets appropriate tension between the spontaneous and the planned ends of the scale when new ideas are recognized and responded to. The system also develops ways to allocate resources, ensures an experiment gets a fair trial, does thoughtful evaluation, and considers the amount of change or experimentation the organization can handle.

Strategies to Move from Excess at the Spontaneous End of the Scale

We see very little of this excess in the largest congregations. Competing interests require large congregations to plan. If you have many committees, many staff, and many programs, each can easily get in the way of the others. The youth fellowship can plan a retreat the same weekend the music department has scheduled the youth choir to sing in the Sunday worship service. The women's organization wants to set up the gym for a second-hand sale, interfering with the aerobics class that meets there every weekday morning. These organizational realities force larger congregations to pay attention to planning.

Smaller congregations, interestingly enough, do not see themselves doing planning, unless they set goals at a planning retreat. Actually they do a good deal of planning by default. Informally and tacitly members know what is expected at each season—at Christmas, at Easter, in the summer. If someone tries to change the usual rota of activities ("Let's not do daily vacation church school this summer"), this may upset some because "We have always had a vacation church school." Just because people do not sit down and plan out a summer schedule each year does not mean that the program is not planned. Doing things the same way, staying in the same patterns, using the same evaluation techniques ("Did you enjoy yourself? How many people showed up? How much did we go in the hole?") is good evidence that the church is actually operating out of the planned end of the scale—though it may perceive itself to be spontaneous.

Here are some ideas about what might be done to move toward the planned end of the scale.

Engage in a Management by Objectives Planning Process

In the 1960s, Peter Drucker came up with this idea of encouraging workers to tell their supervisors what they would like to accomplish in their work and then to negotiate realistic expectations. This process helps the larger organization consider its needs (for profit, coordinating resources, goal accomplishment), and it helps the worker tell the system what is realistic, what is possible.

Using this process, an organization helps its various parts think about what is possible and what is expected before people engage in activities to accomplish the work. When people in the organization agree on their goals and how they will be measured, they are clearly moving into the planned end of the spectrum.

This Management by Objectives (MBO) process does not have to be limited to manufacturing or sales organizations. It can also be applied to voluntary systems. We have been involved in the development of several MBO planning systems in congregations and judicatories. First, we asked the board to set general goals for the church. Then, based on those goals, staff and committees are asked to write specific objectives to be accomplished by a certain time. Once the objectives are written, there is a discussion among the board and the committees or staff to get clarity about those objectives. At the end of the implementation period, the committees and staff who have been carrying out the work evaluate their progress toward the goals and objectives; what has hindered and helped that progress, and what will they do in the next implementation period?

On the following page are some examples of agendas for setting objectives in an Episcopal diocese.

Committees Design for Generating Objectives

FOR SETTING OBJECTIVES YOU WILL NEED:

Goals and Mission Statement of the Diocese
Information about available resources (estimated income, volunteer/
    paid time available)
Needs and trend reports
Policy decisions that might influence plans
This year's budget (for comparative purposes)
Evaluation of last year's work

OBJECTIVE-SETTING PROCESS

1. Read and share your understanding of the goals and priorities assigned
    to your group. You're not being asked to agree or disagree with the
    goals and priorities. The process is to generate objectives in relation to
    the goals allocated to your committee or agency. There will always be
    more work to be done than you can possibly do. You are obliged only
    to do your best at what you are able to do.
2. Brainstorm objectives you would like to do.
3. Review what has been done in the past. Review what yet needs to be
    done and has not been done, review what finances you have available,
    and what time you have from staff and volunteers.
4. Add any further objectives that come to the group's attention.
5. Given what you know about the needs and urgency in the diocese and
    available resources, select those objectives you believe your group can
    carry out. Some criteria that others have used for choosing objectives
    are:
          Legitimate for our group to do
          Important, needed
          Resources available for implementation
          Some are committed to following through with the task
    You may wish to write your own criteria before making selections.
6. Refine each possible objective until you have one that meets the
    criteria for an objective, that is...
          It indicates who is responsible for carrying out the task
          It is measurable
          It is specific
          It is achievable
          There is a date by which the task will be accomplished
    An objective usually takes this form: "Who will do what, to what
    extent, by when."
7. Identify the activities that your group will need to undertake to ac-
    complish your objective(s). Plan the activity, carefully including human
    resources (what people are needed, as well as what experience and

expertise), what materials are needed (equipment, supplies, etc.), how much time it will take (how long, beginning and ending when), authority (who is responsible for what), money (how much must be allocated to get the job done).

8.   Identify the success indicators for this activity. By what evidence will you know that you are moving toward the objective? How will you know your activity is on track?

9.   Implement.

Evaluating a Committee's Work

There are two kinds of evaluation, summative (assessment) and formative (development). Summative evaluation is a summary or the sum of all the work that you have done. It adds up the results or products of your work. Formative evaluation asks the question "How could we do better what we have just done?" Formative evaluation is future oriented. Summative evaluation is past oriented. Formative evaluation is the most important kind for the growth and development of your committee. Summative evaluation helps the diocese know what has been accomplished.

The Planning Committee requests that you do summative evaluation for the diocese. At the end of the program year answer these questions:

What have we accomplished this program year?
Are our accomplishments related to our goals and priorities?
What needs to be done next year based on the objectives we have not reached this year?

The formative evaluation done by the committee is to stay within your committee to be used in improving your working processes and relationships. We recommend that you address this task in the following way:

1.   Make a list of all the programs you have done this year.

2.   Identify all the results that have come out of these programs, both those that are intended and those that came serendipitously.

3.   Based on the success indicators you established at the beginning of the year, show where you were successful, where you were not successful, and where you were partially successful.

4.   Review the strengths and weaknesses of your processes over the past year and make recommendations for how your work together next year can be improved.

The Planning Committee will then review the summative evaluation of all the committees so that the diocese will know what the church has accomplished this year and, also, what needs to be done next year. The planning committee will compare the goals and priorities set for this program year to the products and needs that are identified. It will then prepare a revision of the goals and priorities for the next year to present to the diocese.

Reduce the Size of Planning Groups

Limiting the participation of people in the planning process does not necessarily guarantee tighter (less spontaneous) planning, but it is easier to control the planning process if there is limited participation from various sectors of the organization. In organizations that have complicated tasks to accomplish (where high coordination among the parts is needed), the planning becomes more manageable if you limit the number of opinions put into it.

Develop a Core Plan

Having many priorities usually means the organization cannot monitor them. Set only a few priorities. Considering the limited amount of time most church boards spend in meetings and the amount of attention they pay to the various parts of the organization, the system can end up being spontaneous because there is too much information to be handled by the system in any kind of a planned way.

Evaluate Church "Reality" and Compare It with Established Goals

Evaluate the work that gets done. Evaluation calls the attention of the organization to the relationship between goals and plans and what is actually happening. This evaluation is a planning activity. One cannot brainstorm when thinking about what has actually been done and relating that to ways of improving. Brainstorming moves an organization away from planning; evaluating moves it toward planning.

S. L.

CHAPTER VIII

Moving Out of Excess: The Authority Scale

Authority has to do with both the right to make decisions and competence and experience. A congregation can get stuck at the concentrated end of the scale by locating expertise only in a few people or by insisting that all decisions must go through a certain individual or committee or certain power brokers.

Strategies to Move from Excess at the Concentrated End of the Scale

It is not unusual to see congregations in excess at the concentrated end of the authority scale. Sometimes the pastor makes sure that all decisions go through her; sometimes she spends so much time doing the tasks herself (and so little time involving others in the decision-making process) that, *de facto,* she ends up being the authority on all matters related to the church.

Some denominations structure congregations in a more concentrated way than others. In these congregations the right to make decisions is pretty much kept (by canon law or the constitution) to the clergy or a small group. This does not necessarily mean that concentrated authority is lodged in those who give the church the most time or those who are legally responsible for the organization. Authority might have fallen into the hands of one or a few because others took little or no responsibility. Or a person (or persons) might have been so loud, so bizarre, that others did not know how to say no.

Decreasing concentrated authority in any organization is difficult, at best. Those who have authority don't give it up easily; those who challenge it flag quickly; those who find their power increasing tend to take on more concentrated authority for themselves, finding that road easier than maintaining a more dispersed authority system. With all these warnings, let's look at some tactics that can help disperse concentrated authority.

Enlarge Committee Size

If one can get more people involved in thinking about what is happening and help them stay at the task of thinking about what they are doing, one has a chance of dispersing the authority to a larger group of people. But enlarging committees can work against the dispersal of authority if a group gets too large. Large groups (twelve or more) tend to allow subgroups to do the hard thinking—taking the initiative, which again concentrates authority.

Involve New People in Boards and Committees

Just increasing the size of a decision-making group can move a system toward the dispersal of authority. But even more unsettling of concentrated authority is putting new, uninformed people in positions. Of course, you can go too far on this strategy, just as you can with enlarging the committee. If people are too new, too insecure, or too uneducated in the lore and ways of the congregation, they are likely to let the older hands lead, and the advantage of newness can be lost.

The advantage of being new to a system is that one doesn't yet know the tacit contracts. The beginner sees aspects of the congregation others don't see. The greenhorn notices the dingy carpet, how difficult it is to get into the church office on a week day, how he was treated by the congregation that thinks it is the friendliest church in town. The rookie doesn't know whom she is supposed to check with, what the proper way to do things is, indeed might even bring fresh ideas and opinions to the discussion of what needs to be done.

Shorten Tenure on Boards, Committees

Long tenure in leadership positions works against dispersed authority. If people who have been doing the work are willing to continue, the path of least resistance is to help them carry on in those roles. Congregations don't try very hard to recruit leadership. Unless the organization is "forced" to find someone else to do this work, those who have been doing it will be allowed to continue—out of courtesy, appreciation, or resistance to the effort required to recruit, train, and supervise new people.

Increase the Number of People Consulted before Decisions Are Made

Sometimes it is not easy or possible because of denominational polity to increase the size of a committee, but decision makers can find ways to consult others before making a final decision. Churches do this commonly: Send out a survey to the members, ask people to come to congregational meetings to hear proposals, have small groups meet in homes to discuss in depth the concerns of the day.

Establish Program Priorities to Develop New Areas of Expertise and Authority

This strategy can be delicate. Those who have been in authority are not likely to be impressed with other "new" ways of doing things or priorities. Often this expansion into new program, new expertise, and new authority is threatening to the powers that be.

A frequent scenario in congregations is where some members have encountered a stimulating, meaningful, exciting, energy-producing experience. Perhaps it was a lay witness weekend, a mission trip to Mexico, or a family camp at the denominational conference center. These people become enthusiastic about their new-found wisdom, skill, friendships, or insights, and they take it to others in the congregation. Their zeal empowers them; their practice of the new faith, the new processes—the new whatever—makes it possible for them to challenge the way things have been going. This challenge can be threatening to the rest of the church (or some in the congregation), or the leaders can make room for this new fervor in the life of the congregation. "Making room" automatically means that authority is being dispersed, that other centers of power are developing.

Empower Other Committees

Take some responsibilities from one or more boards and give them to other committees. This is a development of the strategy of involving new people on boards and committees and expanding the size of committees. Giving others new responsibilities can very well disperse authority in the congregation.

Worship committees make an interesting topic of study. Some worship committees are established by seemingly democratic clergy who notice that the last pastor didn't have a worship committee. The new pastor sets up a new committee but then gives it little or no responsibility and uses it only as a council of advice when trying to decide how to get people to pay for new hymnals or paraments. Without responsibility, without regular meetings, without well-educated committee members, the authority stays concentrated in the hands of the one who does the work, the one who makes the decisions.

Boards that are responsible for everything leave the power concentrated in the hands of a few because it is not possible (in terms of discussion and reflection time) for all the subjects to be discussed and understood adequately. In reality, the authority remains in the hands of the few who are finally responsible for and make the decisions.

Meet More Often

The more often a board or committee meets, the more knowledgeable all its members become. Irregular or widely spaced meetings keep board members dependent on the few who can keep up with the day-to-day activities and lore of the group for which it is responsible.

The board of one congregation kept authority dispersed by meeting twice a month. At one meeting the members attended to the administration of the congregation: budget, goals, personnel, and program. At the second meeting the members listened to reports from one another about what was happening in the congregation. Each board member was asked to be in touch with a cell-group leader (cell groups met weekly in members' homes) or the leader of a congregational committee to find out what the group was doing, what the needs of members were, and how the board could be helpful. About half of this meeting was spent hearing from the various cell groups and committees; the other half was not spent in planning and budgeting but in praying for each other and the work of the church.

Take Decisions to Other Parts of the Organization for Approval

Of course, the more levels of approval one has in the organization, the more dispersed the authority. If one does not have to get others' approval, the authority is, by definition, concentrated.

Create Cross-functional Task Forces

This is a handy tool for dealing with special concerns that affect more than one part of the organization at a time. Sometimes the governing board wants to take over this kind of issue, but there can be real advantage to two groups (each of which has some stake in the outcome of a decision) establishing a task force made up of some members of each group to carry out a task. (Notice that this creates a third center of power impacting on the decision: the two original groups and the task force.)

This worked well for a congregation that wanted to hire both a volunteer coordinator and a person to work with the youth group. The church felt it could afford to pay for only a part-time person in each position, and they thought it might be possible to combine the two responsibilities in one person. So the youth committee (a subcommittee of the Christian education committee) and the deacons (who had come up with the idea of the volunteer coordinator) each sent three people to the task force. These people were to come back with recommendations, first about the job description and needed qualifications and then about potential candidates.

**Use a Participatory Process to Get Agreement
on the Church's Focus**

This strategy is a generalized process to involve many people in the processes of decision making, especially on the mission and vision of the
church. Getting more people to think about what the congregation
should be doing can empower members around interests that may not
have been developed (or have been inadequately developed) up to this
point.

Strategies to Move from Excess at the Dispersed End
of the Scale

As many congregations experience trouble at the dispersed end of the
authority scale as at the concentrated end. "Who's in charge around
here? We just can't seem to make a decision; if one person is opposed to
an action, the board is afraid to make the decision." Synagogues and
congregational and Baptist churches seem to suffer from this malady
more than more hierarchically oriented institutions. But dispersed (tacit)
authority structures can be found even in the formal structures of a
Methodist or Catholic church.

When a congregation is unable to make decisions or carry them out
once they have been voted, it may well be that it is suffering from
rigidity at the dispersed end of the authority scale.

Set Priorities for Ministry

Priorities can function as the "elite" of a congregation, if the congregation pays attention to them. Churches with congregational polity can set
goals (involving many members in the process) and then keep those
goals before the staff, the committees, and the parish as a whole.

Those who are leery about hierarchy may lose some of their rigidity
if they have been seriously engaged in the process of planning and setting the priorities of the congregation.

Congregations without goals are particularly vulnerable to authority
getting lodged in individuals or committees rather than in the larger

system because the system has few or no criteria to express the will of the larger group. The leadership in a congregation with goals set by the congregation is challenged to be more responsive to the larger group than to individuals in authority.

Reduce Committee Size

Here you see the opposite advice to that given above for reducing the concentration of authority. Smaller groups have more ability than large groups to communicate in depth about their concerns. The individual members become more expert, more experienced, and more able to lead as their personal authority increases and their numbers decrease.

Meet Less Often, for Shorter Periods

When a church holds its board and committee meetings on week nights at 5:00 or 5:30, participants usually want to get home to dinner and may not be interested in probing the depths of organizational questions. This puts increased power in the hands of the staff, who are able to prepare for the meetings. Staff members become the authorities on the issues, and the board (if it doesn't really know the issues) loses some of its power to shape the congregation meaningfully.

Denominational systems that have the most dispersed authority often have congregational meetings frequently; some meet every week after church on Sunday. The less often the congregation meets, the less often the board meets, the more concentrated the authority.

Give Longer-Term Assignments

Long-term assignments increase members' expertise and their ownership in the task. Short-term assignments take authority out of the activity. One way the U.S. Navy keeps ship captains from becoming a law unto themselves is to move them from command to command every year to eighteen months. This puts the authority in the rules rather than in the people.

Develop a Recruiting Process that Identifies Competencies of Members; Match Expertise with Needs

To more powerfully increase members' authority, put people in jobs they want to do, jobs they are good at. Many congregations these days are hiring volunteer coordinators tasked with finding out what people in the congregation can do, where they want to grow in their spiritual journey, what opportunities they are looking for in terms of their personal and professional development (that is, volunteer coordinators find out what people really want to do–not just what they are willing to do). These coordinators also look carefully at the needs of the church and the community and then match people to positions, activities, and growth experiences and actively help members discover and develop their gifts. People who get involved in a part of a congregation where they know they can do well and where they feel confident of the value of the involvement generally take their volunteering seriously and are motivated to become authorities in their areas of expertise.

Give People with Expertise Authority and Responsibility

Expertise rather than longevity can be a measure of authority. This strategy relates to the previous one above. Helping members to discover their interests and then helping them develop their skills will enhance their authority. You can concentrate authority by adding organizational authority and responsibility to their acquired competence.

Discourage Reworking Proposals Brought to Boards by Committees

The more the church involves others in critiquing, examining, and improving the work of others, the more it will disperse authority in the system.

S. L.

CHAPTER IX

Moving Out of Excess: The Process Scale

Process has to do both with communications and decision making. This scale measures the extent to which ways of communicating and making decisions are clear, regularized, and routine—or flexible, situational, and designed to fit each special situation.

An organization in excess at the mandatory end of this scale is generally unable to find and use processes appropriate to a particular situation; rather, it uses processes that it knows to be "right." At the other end of the scale is the organization that flounders each time it needs to communicate or make a decision. It finds itself involved in long, involved discussions, not only about the issue, but about how to move ahead procedurally.

Strategies to Move from Excess at the Mandatory End of the Scale

Assess the Amount of Control Brought to Bear in the Organization

Such an assessment is not an easy task. It might seem like it shouldn't be too difficult to sit down with friends and talk about the nonconscious rules that govern our behavior. But because the rules are tacit, we don't see them; they are difficult to bring to our consciousness. A stranger or a newcomer will more likely see what is going on than will those who are in the system. Those who are in the system have learned not to notice–to overlook the overcontrol or the chaos.

We did a study of the way churches welcome newcomers into their fellowship. We found that when we asked members to interview newcomers and the newcomers expressed difficulty in entering the church, the members would argue with them or discount the difficulty or simply not hear it. For the interviewers to perceive what the newcomers were actually saying, we had to enlist "interviewers" from another congregation. They had less at stake in making sure that this was a friendly church; they had not been acculturated to accepting "that's the way it is around here," and they were much less likely to blame the newcomer for making it difficult for the members of the church to get to know him or her.

Because of these difficulties in being able to perceive what is going on at the tacit level in an organization, you might bring in an outsider to help the insiders get an accurate view of communications and decision-making processes. When this is not possible (or practical), some work can be done by the organizational members. Usually this works best with small groups of people who have consciously, deliberately practiced the skills of (1) telling the truth and (2) seeing what is going on.

Here are some truth-telling exercises. Talk about things in your life that have impacted your faith journey positively; talk about things that have impacted your faith journey negatively. Tell about a disappointment in your life. Tell about a time you felt powerless. Give another person in the group some feedback on his or her behavior that has impacted you negatively. These exercises, of course, do not get to the heart of what is going on in an organization, but they do help the participants develop skills (and muscle) to feel more confident in situations that otherwise would have been frightening. (Once the group feels more confident in its "truth-telling" abilities, you can move the topic of conversation to authority and control in the congregation.)

You will know the group is gaining confidence in its truth-telling capabilities when its members are able to take risks and not lose their confidence and ability to participate appropriately; when they are able to help one another maintain appropriate boundaries, stay on task, and affirm and support one another when they get nervous and begin to withdraw or become aggressive.

To practice the skills of telling the truth and taking risks in groups, use exercises where people reveal things about themselves they would not ordinarily reveal in a group. Speaking the unspeakable is our goal as we move toward talking about organizational behavior that we have not been given permission to talk about.

To raise the consciousness of the membership, ask people to identify the unwritten rules about how one is to behave in the congregation. Then the group (or groups) can do an analysis of the tacit rules that are helpful to the congregational processes and those that get in the way of smooth op-eration. Again, this has to be done with preparation. People have to feel (and be) safe to talk about the norms or tacit rules of the congregation.

Help Leadership Become Aware of the Effects of Overcontrolling Policies

Often the symptoms of overcontrolling policies—mandatory process— are obvious. Someone becomes upset; group participation dwindles; people talk more, and with more candor, outside of the meetings than they do in the meetings. And sometimes the symptoms are more subtle: Members are quiet; they share only superficial thoughts and feelings; there is never any question about how to approach a given problem because every problem is approached the same way. As people begin to see these problems, their discussion of them can include not only the fact that something needs to be done, but they can also develop strategies to deal with the problems.

Interrupt the Interaction Patterns

Break the rules of the system. This suggestion is tricky. Be careful when you use it. It is tricky because people don't take kindly to those they believe don't know how to act. If the members can see that breaking the rules can improve relationships or communication, then people will be better able to handle the tension of the disrupted homeostasis.

Recontract: Renegotiate the Rules of the System

An easier (and fairer) way to approach the rules of the system is to call together those who notice (or those who can be helped to understand) the impact of the rules on individuals and the organization. Discuss with these people your perceptions and ask for theirs. Make sure you all have a similar understanding of what the tacit or informal rules are and how they impact the functioning of the system. Then seek to find agreements about new ways of being with one another.

Stop Enforcing the Rules

This strategy seems easy enough, but if the rules really are nonconscious and systemic, there usually will be others who will pick up the "enforcing" task and make sure the rules are obeyed. This means it is not good enough for one person or a few people just to stop enforcing the rules. A discussion needs to be held to help the larger group see the value of not enforcing the rules at this time.

Help Make the System More Safe to Challengers

If people feel safer, they will take more risks, and challenging the rules or the processes of a system *is* a risk. To take such a risk, the "challenger" must either have support from within the system or from within himself or herself.

In this strategy, it is probably easier (though still difficult) to change the system—to be a safer place in which to disagree or challenge behavior—than to therapeutically root out the underlying anxieties and fears of individuals. If one can develop a cadre of people who can support one another in the system they are trying to change, who can see the value of the changes, and who can together give leadership—"Come on, we can make it; it will be all right; don't worry; we've been able to do this is the past; we never lost any one in this kind of situation before"—there is a chance that they can successfully encourage people to try another way of operating.

Help Members and Leaders Gain Individual Control
over Their Work

Reduce the amount of "upper-level" review and reworking of decisions made at lower levels of the organization. The more that individuals are choosing to do for themselves or for their part of the organization, the more discretionary the organization is likely to be. It is when churches require elaborate systems for communicating or for getting approval—going through committee after committee—that they go into excess at the mandatory end of this scale.

Work in the "Systems Mode"

Family systems theory says that in some families members feel over-responsible for the others' feelings and behaviors. But family members are not responsible for one another's behavior and/or feelings. The more we try to protect others or make them feel or behave in certain ways, the more powerless we are. We are powerless because it is very difficult to "get" others to feel certain ways or to do certain things. If we feel "called" to straighten another person out, to make sure people have certain experiences or certain feelings, we often put pressure on them to do or feel certain things.

Normally, putting pressure on others to do something increases their resistance—not their readiness to change. Indeed, it usually puts them in a more intransigent position. If I want a person to be closer to me, I might do better to back off than to make advances. Advances beget resistance, backing off invites moving closer.

Trying to "out-authority" the authority is not a very productive strategy for getting a looser rein. Usually this strategy locks the parties into reactive behaviors that lead toward an increasing obstinacy. Various family systems theorists suggest that, instead of trying to pressure others to change, one might pay less attention to them, rather than more. An interesting dimension of authority is that it is not meaningful unless both the leaders and the led agree on who has the authority. Instead of trying to grasp authority from another, one might not pay attention to his or her authoritarian gestures. Not responding can be a way of not cooperating with the system that says, "You're in charge," or, "I don't have anything to say around here."

More effective than passive resistance (which is a subtle version of power play) is turning your interests to something else—not noticing, not responding to the established authority.

Encourage People to Differ

Claiming my own identity and affirming another's identity acknowledges
that the two of us differ. I know I am not you and you know you are not
me. We are differentiating from one another when we choose to know
that we are not the same or don't think the same or don't believe the
same. Here we are not encouraging church members to utterly differ; if
people have nothing in common, they have no relationship. But we
encourage you to explore ways of affirming the polarity of organizational
life: "In this system we have some commonality *and* we differ."

Strategies to Move from Excess at the Discretionary End of the Scale

Help Parties Become Aware of the Effects of Undercontrolling Policies

This kind of strategy has already been mentioned several times. This is
another form of making the nonconscious conscious. Questions to ask:

— What is the cost to the organization when we have to reinvent
  decision-making processes every time we need to make a
  decision?
— What is the cost to the organization when people don't know
  who should be involved in decision making?
— What is the cost to the system when people don't have any idea
  (this time) as to whether this decision should be made by the
  pastor, the council, a committee, or the congregation?

Recontract: Add More Rules to the System

We can recontract to add more rules to the system just as we could recontract to reduce the number of rules in the system. When adding new
rules (especially when the organization is in excess at the discretionary
end of the scale), include sanctions for those who do not follow the rules;

this will have a strong impact on the system. By sanctions we mean consequences. "If you don't do so-and-so, these will be the effects on you, the system, or others."

What would be an example of consequences or sanctions in a religious system? "If we don't have twenty people sign up, we won't hold the course." "We are going to evaluate our decision-making processes at the end of our work so that we can learn from our experience." "We are asking those who are not able to help with the calling at this time to volunteer for the next round of calling."

It is critical that the organization actually follow up on the rules; give feedback and follow through on the sanctions promised for those who do not follow the rules. This sounds parental and judgmental. It does not have to be. It can be adult and affirming. Think of yourself as a diving coach working with a member of the swimming team. The successful coach does not attack members of the team and put them down; she affirms what has been done well and, in the interest not of punishment but of improvement, makes suggestions. "Next time try this. Have you tried that? How can I be helpful to you in dealing with this problem?"

Develop Skills of Members through Training

Training is likely to be the least effective general strategy, but it can be done. It helps change the culture and norms of the system—if you bring on board enough people. Some things one could help people learn to do better:

— giving feedback to one another;
— talking about the value and use of predictable communication and decision-making patterns in the system;
— making decisions using the processes agreed upon in the system.

S. L.

CHAPTER X

Moving Out of Excess: The Leadership Scales

The two leadership scales (pastoral and lay, considered here as a unit) measure the extent to which congregational leaders are looking toward short-term or long-term goals and the extent to which the leaders can tolerate risk. Part of what we will have to say here about strategies for moving from one end of the scale toward the middle of the scale has a good deal to do with (1) the personality characteristics of the leaders and (2) the extent to which the system supports or inhibits a managerial or transformational leadership style. This means that sometimes we will be talking about changing the people in leadership roles and other times we will be directing our attention to the system and the way it functions.

Strategies to Move from Excess at the Managerial End of the Scale

Bring in Transformational Leadership

We will begin by discussing a characteristic of the leader rather than the characteristic of the system. Most congregations have pastors who are more transformational than their lay leadership. If the lay leadership is managerial, a way to keep a managerial-transformational tension in the system is to hire one or more transformational staff members.

If the system cannot manage conflict well, this mix can be problematic. If the system sees bringing in transformational leadership as a signal to fight, having two different styles present in the system will not be helpful. A system in healthy tension will support, encourage, and respect the differing leadership styles.

Some congregations deliberately structure themselves in this way. The laypeople see their role as the nuts and bolts and expect the clergy to be more transformational. For all parties to live with the tension, there must be some kind of an understanding that this is appropriate.

Focus on Long-Term rather than Short-Term Goals

The further into the future a leader or committee looks, the less managerial she, he, or it is likely to be. Congregations that are used to looking at only three- to five-year goals tend to be conservative (managerial) in their thinking because they are rightly asking, "How do we accomplish these goals?" When the planners or leaders are not constrained by this question, they can be more transformational in their thinking.

Do Planning with People Who Are Not on "Maintaining" Committees

This is Lyle Schaller's idea. He says if you want a group to think about new and innovative ideas, do not put people in the group whose roles include being responsible for "keeping the ship afloat," maintaining the smooth functioning of the church. Imaginative thinking is stifled by the legitimate concerns of people functioning in managerial roles within the organization.

Acquaint (Face to Face) Members with People and Needs in the Community or the Membership

We have already discussed this strategy in chapter VII. This kind of experience can be powerful in loosening a system; as members become acquainted with real needs, they can be motivated to challenge conserving instincts that might be based on perceptions that are not based in people's experience.

Sound the Alarm; Capitalize on Environmental Forces

If the managerial leadership of a church can see that what is happening in
the community (change of neighborhood, for example) is negatively
influencing institutional indicators of organizational health (attendance,
membership, or giving, etc.), it may stand up and give some attention to
transformational, long-term sights. "Yes, these long-range concerns do
relate to our short-range concerns." This is another instance of helping
people become newly conscious of specific dimensions of their organizational life.

Strategies to Move from Excess at the Transformational End of the Scale

In churches in excess at the transformational end of the scale (there are
very few of them out there), the leadership can engage in managerial
activities that will increase the possibility of bringing the dreamers down
to earth.

Help Members Understand Roles Needed within the Congregation; Assign Duties, Responsibilities, Evaluation Procedures

This is a very common strategy of managerial leaders: Get clear on who
is supposed to do what by when. The more people talk about these concerns, the more they will be pulled into short-range, risk-management
types of discussion. Ask the board to get agreement on the policies and
procedures of the church and then write a policy manual based on that
agreement.

Focus on Short-Range Planning

Instead of dreaming and thinking about what is going to happen way out
in the future, explore what can be accomplished in the near future. In
excess at the transformational end of the scale, leaders may have their
heads in the clouds and need to think more about the here and now
before they focus on distant tomorrows.

Organize a Board of Trustees
to Oversee Financial-Organizational Management

Some congregations have only a church council. Dividing the council into two parts—one to manage the money, the other to work with program—can force the congregation to focus more on management.

Keep Minutes of Meetings

Keeping minutes of meetings is a managerial task. It helps the group focus on control and is a function of organizational tightness. All tasks that draw the congregation's attention toward order will increase managerial leadership.

In Church Reports Focus on Budget, Control of Facility Use, Evaluation of Staff

Many congregations lose their transformational energy as meetings, annual reports, and informal discussions focus more and more on control or management rather than on the purposes for which the group was organized. Directing attention away from the transformational concerns will move the group toward the managerial. (By "evaluation of staff" we refer to evaluations based on time use and accountability.)

Train Members to Run Meetings

This is really a function of the concerns raised in the preceding paragraph. Developing skill in management will direct people's attention toward management.

Enlarge Planning Committees with People Already Responsible for Maintaining the System

This recommendation is the opposite of the strategy for moving out of transformational excess. The larger the planning group, the more probable that visions will move toward the lowest common denominator. The more people are concerned about the maintenance of the organization, the less transformational they will be.

S. L.

CHAPTER XI

Moving Out of Excess: The Relatedness Scale

The relatedness scale measures the extent to which people work together or alone in the system. How much togetherness do they need? At the collegial end of the scale, people want to check with each other, work together, and meet needs for inclusion. At the individual end of the scale, everyone wants to do his or her own thing—not necessarily working with others or for others, but functioning autonomously. At either end of the scale, one loses the benefits of the other. In the middle of the scale, a congregation has the ability to embrace each value from time to time.

Strategies to Move from Excess at the Collegial End of the Scale

In excess at the collegial end of the scale the organization finds that most tasks are done by people in groups—frequently checking in with one another and constantly trying to reduce difference or conflict. The focus is on getting along (even at the cost of not looking hard at tough issues). Dissent is seen as not being a team player, not as an opportunity to explore new dimensions of a problem. Here are some strategies to pull the organization back toward the individual end of the scale.

Assign Work to Individuals or Committees

Do this especially when the board or a certain group in the congregation is doing all of the work.

Collegiality is an interesting phenomena; the more collegial certain people get, the more others are left out. Often collegiality functions as a barrier to involvement of the many because of the collegiality of a few. The first step toward moving away from excessive collegiality could be—not to have people work alone but—to explore ways to establish several centers of collegiality rather than one or a few. As the congregation begins to see that it can cooperate across various committee identities, it can explore a greater autonomy by encouraging certain tasks to be done by individuals rather than groups. The church might explore giving titles to people who are functioning individually so it is clear that such a role is legitimate; it's not just someone riding a hobby horse. So the congregation may have a vice-president for missions rather than a missionary committee that never meets; or an evangelism consultant rather than an evangelism committee in a church where the function of evangelism is carried out by other existing groups—if it gets done at all.

Assign Work to People Able to Work Alone

Many who do not like to work with groups are excluded from church life. If you are not a committee person, if you like to do things on your own, you may be turned off by the way many churches are structured. The preceding strategy includes some ideas about tasks that can be done alone in the church.[1]

Train People in Conflict Management

Again, the proposal here is to change congregational norms dealing with personal differences *and* to develop individual skills in dealing with challenge and resistance.

People confident about their abilities to deal with challenge generally do so better than those who are not as confident. And people who see a variety of options for dealing with differences also manage conflict better than those who see fight or flight as their two choices.

Identify Conflict Norms and Recontract around Those Norms

These two items go together and have been named in just about every other chapter dealing with strategy for moving out of excess. We won't explore this idea more fully here, except to note that this strategy is especially important when dealing with collegiality. If the organization's only style for being collegial is to suppress conflict or difference, the lack of tolerance for conflict will inhibit the organization's moving out of this excess.

Increase Competition among People or Groups

This reduces collegiality and increases individuality. (This may be true only in the differentiation among the competitive groups. Some competition increases collegiality within groups.)

Is this a wise strategy in churches? Not always. In some excessively collegial congregations, it can create so much discomfort as to be counterproductive. In some situations the competition could become the focus of the life of the congregation, and one would reap the costs of unproductive challenge and counterchallenge. Having said this, there are times when increased competition might function to the benefit of the system. For example:

— Put more than one candidate up for every position in a church election. This encourages discussion of the kind of leadership that is needed and the qualifications of those who will be leading.
— Engage in competition with other congregations. Some congregations tell members that their giving ratio is higher than any other in the denomination or that they are doing better in steward ship than all the other churches in the community.
— In many denominations congregations compete over getting the kind of pastor they want. Clergy compete for positions. Search committees compare candidates against one another.

 Most denominations have people compete for other paid jobs in the church as well. When people do not compete for jobs, such as hiring a secretary from the congregation, there can be a problem getting the best possible candidate; here the collegial style may be working so rigidly that it is difficult to give feedback and correction in the system.

Are these strategies used in churches? Yes, competition for office is usually subtle, so people may believe this is not really competition; it is merely an award ceremony. But when it comes to choosing clergy, congregations choose to be more individual than collegial.

Encourage Individual Initiative

Here we're talking about contests—who comes up with the best idea. Awards might be given for attendance, participation, or leadership. Some might say this is merely recognition, but it also functions to arouse competitive instincts in some parishioners.

You might award prizes or grants to the best proposal for something. The national offices in one denomination have made grants of ten to twenty thousand dollars available to individual congregations willing to try innovative ways to invite and assimilate newcomers. In various parts of the country, this has stimulated interest in church growth developing new ideas for involving members in congregational life.

Stuck at the collegial end of the scale, churches are primarily motivated by "trying to get along." Without some kind of stimulus from the outside to value individuality more than collegiality, the congregation will find it difficult to stir up individual initiative (that is, ways of being different in the organization).

Reward Mistakes as well as Successes

This is an interesting strategy to contemplate in a religious system. A person who contributes to the life of a congregation by volunteering is asked to volunteer more. For some this is a reward. For others it feels like punishment; the costs of volunteering one time outweigh the contribution one is making to the organization. Especially those who do not get satisfaction from working with groups may be worried about agreeing to volunteer for fear they will be asked to volunteer again and again.

There is an often-told story of a business executive of a large computer company who awarded a million dollars to one man to do a special project. The man did the project, but failed to produce the hoped-for result. Because of his failure, the man submitted his resignation. The executive said he would not accept his resignation, but gave him another project because "the company had just invested one million dollars in him and his learning." The executive did not want to lose that invest-ment. If failure is punished, individual initiative (differentiation) is inhibited.

What would this look like in a church system? The kinds of rewards given in religious organizations include recognition, inclusion, authority, and the knowledge that one has been able to contribute meaningfully to the good of the community. If the church does not have means for help-ing people feel successful in meeting their needs (for recognition, inclu-sion, authority, and fulfillment), then individual initiative is likely to be stifled. We have worked in congregations where success is punished as if it were failure. A dinner is held and people feel bad—their endeavor could have been so much better—because only fifty people showed up. Or a great training event is held and the parking lot discussion is about how the people who really needed this did not participate.

What would rewarding failure look like? Partly it would make sure that we learn from our experience. It would see the failure as a gift in some sense; something of value has come from the experience. You can recognize the good the group has gotten from the experience or recog-nize the fact that people have been faithful, even though we have not achieved the goal. In a professional organization we saw members share failures they had experienced in their work and what they learned. These people were rewarded with recognition, authority ("I'm an expert on what not to do!"), and fulfillment ("I can help others avoid the same mis-takes"). If we have to hide our mistakes and problems, individuality is decreased.

Give More Authority to Individuals

Instead of making it necessary for people to check with others before taking initiative or making decisions, within agreed upon parameters encourage people to act on their own. Giving authority is not just giving the right to take initiative and make decisions; it is also recognizing the special gifts and skills that others bring to the organizational life. Helping people become expert at teaching or at helping volunteers find a place in the congregation or at leading worship gives them authority. It sets them apart as individuals.

In general, helping people get training and experience and encouraging them to become even more expert will help the organization move from excess at the collegial end of the scale.

Strategies to Move from Excess at the Individual End of the Scale

Assign Work Done by Individuals to Committees

This is so obvious it hardly needs to be said. If one has a problem with people doing too much individually, make sure the tasks are put into organizational functions delegated to groups. One congregation got themselves into a situation where all the financial information was in the control of one individual. He knew what money was spent for, how much money was needed, and what the congregation was likely to raise. This gave him a great deal of authority in the system. To reduce his authority, a board of trustees was established on which he was asked to be a member. After some rocky beginnings, the trustees were able to actually hold meetings, clarify their task, and get the information they needed to work using the wisdom of the group, in addition to the wisdom of the treasurer.

Start Small-Group Meetings—
Talk about Feelings, Relationships, and Spiritual Journeys

The way a group approaches its task will greatly influence the extent to which it is individually or collegially organized. Encouraging people to talk about the quality of their working relationships, helping them reflect on their feelings as well as their ideas and explore and learn from the processes of their work together—these will help move the focus of congregational life from individual to collegial.

Reduce Competition among Groups

Competition enhances differentiation; cooperation reduces isolation and individuality. See "Increase Competition" earlier in this chapter.

Enable Groups to Work across Functions

This is an often used process to help reduce competition among groups. See chapter VIII, the "Create Crossfunctional Task Forces" strategy, for an example.

Move toward Collaborative Decisions

Instead of encouraging difference, encourage people to understand one another's point of view and find cooperative solutions. Collaboration is, perhaps, the most difficult way to make decisions in groups. It requires that everybody is listened to carefully. All are helped to explore their needs and interests as well as solutions. All are asked to share fully what they know about the subject. (Secrets are not appropriate in collaboration.) Decisions are not made until all agree and all get their needs met. Collaboration focuses on feelings and relationships as well as the issues under discussion.

S.L.

CHAPTER XII

Moving Out of Excess: The Learning Scale

The learning scale measures the extent to which an organization looks to the past or the future as it considers what is most helpful for its growth or survival. At some times in their history, healthy organizations look to the past, asking themselves, "What are our strengths? At what have we been successful?" This is focusing on the maximizing end of the scale. At other times in their history, organizations ask, "What can we do differently? Do these times call for a new strategy or an experiment to help us grow or survive?"

As we have said repeatedly in this book, both kinds of learning are important for congregational life. One can focus too much on the experimental or too much on the glories of the past and present. A healthy system needs the ability to move from one to the other—the ability to use successes but also to take some risks, do things differently, and attempt to find new ways of adapting to the environment.

Strategies to Move from Excess at the Maximizing End of the Scale

If your congregation is not able to get out of a mindset that focuses on the past, "We need a women's group like we had in the fifties," or on its strengths, "What we know how to do best is preaching and worship, so let's cut back on program and do better what we already do well," then you may want to help the leadership explore ways to experiment and look at the future. Here are some suggestions.

Take Planning Group through Envisioning Exercises

This is probably the most common way for congregations to try to break out of thinking in old patterns. But one has to be careful lest people envision that the future will look like the "golden age" of the church forty years ago. We did an envisioning exercise with a congregation where we asked people to close their eyes and imagine that they could fly on a magic carpet into the future. They were to look at the church two years from now, five years from now, and ten years from now, and then make notes about what their imagination saw in the church of the future. Most saw things the same as they were now (only more so—larger groups, more money, higher frequency of attendance).

For the envisioning process to avoid choosing a past "golden age," it is necessary at least for people to experience new ways of thinking, new ways of doing. We encourage groups to read or in some other way expose themselves to new ideas (that is, new ideas to them). Brainstorming with only one's personal past as foundational preparation is not likely to produce new ideas. If people have been given a chance to explore other ideas by reading a book or a chapter that describes what other successful churches have done, she or he might have an idea about how those experiences or one of those experiences might impact the life of this congregation. We have worked with congregations that send out teams to other churches to discuss what they have done in the way of ministry or structure. Once the teams have had experience with new or different ways of approaching problems, they can begin their brainstorming.

Recruit Leaders with New Ideas

This has been mentioned several times before. See page 86.

Put New Members on Program Committees

Sometimes it helps to add to the mix of those exploring "what might be done"; add people other than those ordinarily involved in the process. Taking members of the church into the community or into new environments can help them see the world and themselves from a new perspective, breaking the old thinking patterns and encouraging new ideas in

situations that require new perspectives. Many times when a congregation faces a rapidly declining youth group, they decide that what they
need is a new youth leader—someone young. Then they go out and hire
one. But one congregation started at another place. First they put six
young people on the youth study committee. Then they trained themselves to gather information from young people about the issues they
were facing at home, at school, in the community, and in their faith journey. This committee (in pairs) not only interviewed young people whose
families were active in the church, but they went to the high school, to
Mel's Drive-In (and two other hang-outs) on a Friday evening, and to a
national denominational conference on youth ministry.

In this situation the reader can see that when the committee members began to explore new ideas, they greatly increased the likelihood
that they would be able to metamize rather than maximize; they had
broadened their experience of the world.

Another way to approach this idea of envisioning is to use a process
that challenges the individual or group to break through the unconscious
barriers that keep us from getting in touch with our creativity. A number
of available techniques help people tap their creativity, moving away
from maximizing to metamizing. One such technique we have used is
the practice of Synectics.[1] George Prince, the developer of this approach
to creative thinking, uses special techniques employing metaphor, special
group processes, and what he calls the "Force Fit" technique to break
through stuck places. Prince's techniques are too complex to include
here. Yet the use of processes such as his can greatly enhance a
congregation's metamizing.

Establish Experimental Programs

It is not enough for a church just to tolerate new programs. Nor is it
enough to brainstorm. Most of us have spent an evening or a weekend
dreaming about the future. We come up with more ideas than we can
even hold in our heads. They seem remote, risky, expensive, outrageous.
We postpone any actual decisions on the ideas until a later date and find
they never make it back into a slot on the priority agenda for the church.
For a new idea to work, it has to be implemented. Before any project
actually happens, there must be a budget, people willing to do the work,
space, and resources. If a congregation is going to experiment with

metamizing, it must commit enough resources to the project to get it past
the awkward first failures and disappointments of the idea. Of course,
there are times when failures need to be abandoned—but not until the
idea has been tried several different ways, and the participants have had
a chance to learn from their experience. (That's the whole idea of
metamizing.)

Engage in Faith Development Activities

The use of silence, meditation, contemplation, and reflection can be
powerful ways of expanding our perception of the options open to us. If
the individual or committee relies only on what she, he, or it can do with
what seems to be available resources, it would certainly be wise to minimize one's risk. But if perspective includes a faith that we are not alone,
new resources are possible, and new possibilities for our church are in
sync with the will of God. If this is our faith perspective, we have an
added strength to move toward being more venturesome, taking more
risks.

Encourage Groups Developing Strategies to Proceed without Asking Permission

Use Lyle Schaller's idea of "only counting the 'yes' votes." That is,
allow people who want to do something to go ahead and do it, even without a majority vote. Sometimes we structure our organization in such a
way (authority is either too dispersed or concentrated) that we empower
those who don't catch the vision (this can be a minority or a majority) to
stop those who do have a vision. Excesses at the maximizing end of the
scale are abetted by concentrated authority, especially that which perceives itself as responsible for the preservation and management of the
system.

Challenge Norms That Discourage Debate and Initiative

Debate is necessary if a group is to move out of excess at the maximizing
end of the learning scale. When discussion or debate is curtailed, it is

usually because the norms of the system are inhibiting dialogue and constraining experimentation. Without discussion, an organization generally will not attempt to do things differently. One might begin this process not by dealing with maximizing directly, but by helping people learn conflict management skills. As the people in the group learn to differ with one another (or perhaps get used to differing), they can better handle the tension of experimentation within the organization.

It is interesting to note how frequently organizations have norms that punish people for taking initiative. If it is necessary to check with many levels of the system before taking initiative, if people who challenge old ways of doing things are ostracized, made fun of, or penalized in other ways, the norms will function to inhibit metamizing behavior.

Encourage a Discussion of the "Tyranny of Successful Habits"

The reader will recall our earlier discussion of this tyranny. In chapter I we spoke of "tunnel vision" and the need for congregations to be able to respond to present need. Unless the congregation (or its leaders) becomes aware of the present needs of its members or of those it wishes to serve, it will keep doing what it has been doing, rather than shifting to more experimental possibilities. Here "consciousness raising" is the key—raising awareness of how the congregation and its leaders have been blind to the need to change, relying on past success.

Strategies to Move from Excess at the Metamizing End of the Scale

We rarely find congregations stuck at the metamizing end of the scale. The largest congregations (Corporate-sized) tend to do a better job of working at the tension than smaller congregations, but not many of these are in excess at the metamizing end. If it is necessary to slow the experimentation down, here are some useful strategies.

Assess What Has Worked Well in the Recent Past

This is the opposite planning strategy from the one presented to move a group away from the tight end of the learning scale. In this case, You ask questions about the past rather than the future.

Kennon Callahan's very good book on church planning is an excellent resource for building on the strengths of a congregation. He wisely cautions churches at the metamizing end of the scale against trying to do too much new, too fast.[2]

Instead of dreaming dreams, look at the present and recent paths. Ask what is it that you do well? Why is it that people are now coming to the church? What is your specialty as a congregation? Going back over the congregation's recent history to assess numerical successes, see where it has given people quality experiences, where it has accomplished much with little effort. The church might want to center in on these areas to do even better.

Get the Approval of Large Numbers of People before Proceeding on Any Course

Metamizing is by its nature risky and likely to be resisted by most people. It is easier to see the value of maximizing, i.e., doing what works. This means that broadening the base of participation in decision making is likely to increase maximizing and decrease metamizing.

Establish Rules That Programs not Be Changed for X Years after Implementation

Flighty management (metamizing to excess) doesn't give new ideas a chance. Use the strengths of maximizing to make sure that programs are run responsibly, reducing risk, providing resources, and planning the next steps carefully.

Connect Vision to Clear, Specific Goals

When envisioning, make sure that your planning group attends carefully not just to the new ideas that would be really great, but also to the nitty-gritty: Who will do what, how much, and by when?

Build a Sequenced Plan That Stretches over Several Years

This will enable leaders to stay with the pursuit of goals.

Create a "Parking Lot" for Creative Ideas

In such a "parking lot" ideas are not lost, but neither are they acted upon. If the leadership of a congregation that gets excited about every new idea that comes down the road squelches the ideas ("That sounds good, we'll get to it later"), people will be disheartened and think ideas are forgotten—unless there is a place where they can go and look at them from time to time. Some groups use an agenda page to keep track of ideas they need to return to in the future. Others have a placard or use newsprint to keep track of ideas so they don't get lost. (Before you set ideas aside in this "parking lot," you might want to write them out in paragraph form. A phrase-list may not communicate much if it is read again after six months or a year.)

Conclusion

Many of these strategies, presented in chapters VII through XII, can be used in combination with others, and some work to change more than one organizational dimension. (Strategies related to movement from the managerial end of the leadership scale and the planning end of the strategy scale are particularly linked.)

As you try to move from any excess, don't try to do too much too fast. Like salt in the soup, it doesn't take much to flavor the batch.

                                                                            S. L.

CHAPTER XIII

Profile Statistics

Generalizations about Congregations

From the scores of all 515 lay and clergy leaders who filled out inventories on their congregations, we can draw some conclusions about the "average" church. Since this data includes all sizes of congregations and many different denominations, we are hesitant to draw sweeping conclusions from this information. Yet there are some trends of interest.

On the following page are the scores of an average congregation. (Remember, a 0 score is extremely ordered, a 10 score is extremely loose. This scale graphs only from 1 to 7.)

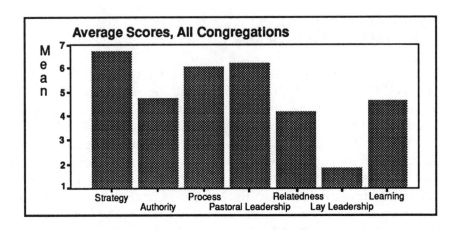

Lay Leadership	1.89
Relatedness	4.01
Learning	4.57
Authority	4.63
Process	5.96
Pastoral Leadership	6.11
Strategy	6.71

Lay and Pastoral Leadership

According to the lay leadership assessments of both laity and clergy, the laity are in excess at the managerial end of the scale. This is the only average score in excess. We read this to mean that the laity see their responsibility as being: to keep the ship afloat, to reduce risk taking, to plan for short-term goals, and to ensure that necessary resources are available before the church undertakes a new task. Comparing these low lay leadership scores with the significantly higher pastoral leadership (i.e., transformational) scores, one can see a potential for creative tension! These scores do not necessarily mean that clergy and laity are destined for trouble, but if clergy think laity are "wrong" for being managerial and laity think clergy are "wrong" for being transformational, the stage is set for significant organizational difficulty. The key here is in seeing (understanding) that each role is legitimate; each role is necessary. A healthy system must tolerate this difference in its functioning. When the system loses its ability to tolerate good managerial leadership and good transformational leadership, it has become rigid or gotten itself into a fight.

In a conflicted system the opponents have lost the ability to see the value of the other's cause, the other's role, the other's perception. Losing sight of this value, the sides lock on to each other (often ridiculously), shutting out half of what is needed for organizational health.

It is best when an organization does not incarnate managerial roles in certain people or offices and transformational roles in other people or offices—when this managerial-transformational tension is embodied in the entire board and the pastor. Here neither group tends to see the other as enemy. Keeping the ambiguity in all parts of the system decreases the likelihood of out-of-control conflict.

Relatedness

The average score for relatedness approaches the rigid "collegial" end of the scale. It looks as if congregations like to do most of what they have to do together. This probably makes it uncomfortable for those who don't like "togetherness" to find a place in a religious system. A congregational norm that says, "It won't get done, if we don't do it together," will significantly reduce the participation of those who don't like "groupy" activities. This also will impact the style of organizational life. Congregations entrenched at the collegial end of the scale tend to be conflict avoiders—with strong aversion to anything that might cause tension in a relationship, that is, reduce relatedness. A congregation operating out of the collegial end of the scale frequently sees only collaborative and consensus options for decision making and sometimes loses the ability to make decisions efficiently and quickly or to give decisions over to those who may be more expert than the group.

Strategy

In the average congregation there is pretty good tension in the areas of learning, authority, process, and pastoral leadership. Strategy, however, is pushing close to excess at the spontaneous end of the scale. We have noticed that many congregations engage in formal planning. They have annual retreats where goals are set; they write profiles of the congregation before hiring new staff. The problem is that the planning is merely formal; it is not also tacit. The board may say its number-one goal is evangelism, but that doesn't mean anyone (except a few marginal people) takes that seriously. The goals get set and then forgotten, or they are not used to determine budget, allocation of the staff's time, or programming.

Summary

What then can we say about an average church? The laity and the clergy have some tension about the extent to which the church is supposed to take risks and the extent to which it is to be managed. People like to work together in groups. They are not really sure how to make decisions, and they don't do much planning that is used for managing the organization.

Congregational Size Theory and the CSI Data

Several years ago Arlin Rothauge developed a very useful theory for differentiating the size of congregations.[1] Rothauge divides congregations into four sizes based on average Sunday morning attendance:

The Family Church:	fewer than 50 average attendance
The Pastoral Church:	50-150 average attendance
The Program Church:	150-350 average attendance
The Corporate Church:	more than 350 average attendance

For each of the four categories, we will describe Rothauge's theory using material on assimilation of new members published by The Alban Institute[2] and then explore other differences that may be noticed according to church size.

First, this graph shows the differences in average CSI scores, grouping congregations by size.

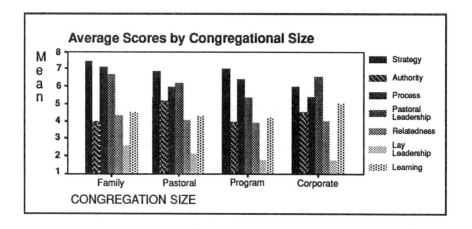

Family-Sized Congregations

According to Rothauge the smallest congregations are most likely to be made up of what sociologists call a cell. Carl Dudley defines a cell: "...members are united by common interest, beliefs, tasks and territory. They are not self-conscious about their relationships and are bound together more by sentimental ties than by contractual agreements. They have a solidarity, a feeling of belonging, nourished by experiences of intimacy and personal need.[3]

This cell is very much like a family and usually provides a social place for members that includes a hierarchy and differentiation of roles. Rothauge claims that one or more people will emerge to fill the roles of leader (matriarch or patriarch) and "gatekeeper."

A couple (or one person) joining a Family-size Church will not find the anonymity one experiences when joining a large social organization. Rothauge observes that a couple joining a Family Church really is being "adopted." The church does the choosing more than the new person does. Joining a Family Church might also be compared to "marrying into" a clan. Those already in the clan spend time getting to know you; they have a lot to say about who you are and how you will fit in. You will not be "in" until others in the clan have had a chance to get used to you and to assess the effect of your presence on individuals and the whole.

Newcomers in a Family Church often encounter a "gatekeeper," one who welcomes the newcomer and helps that person become acquainted. In small congregations, however, newcomers will probably not feel a part of the group until the matriarch or patriarch has made it clear to the newcomer and the rest of the congregation that this new person is on the inside.

New pastors in very small congregations often experience this phenomenon as well. Some congregations never do let the pastor in. Members assume that pastors come and go; they are strangers in town who didn't grow up here and probably won't stay. Not only is it difficult for the members to open up with their pastor, it is also likely that the matriarch or patriarch will not give a full stamp-of-approval to this newcomer (even though she or he is paid to be there).

People who enter Family-size congregations and stay usually have other family or friendship ties in the congregation. Those without these ties usually don't have the persistence to hang around long enough to be adopted.

Our CSI data about Family-size congregations are quite sketchy. Only seventeen congregations in the sample were of this size, and sixteen were Unitarian Universalist (UUA), so we cannot know if we are measuring the characteristics of small churches or the characteristics of small UUA congregations.

With regard to the process CSI category dimension, it looks as if Family-size congregations are more discretionary than the other three sizes. Indeed, when it comes to process, there was a significant[4] difference between each of the four sizes in the following order (see the statistics for this on page 131):

PROCESS

Mandatory   Discretionary

Corporate Pastoral Program Family

It is interesting to speculate why the Family-size congregations are more discretionary than the other sizes. This may be because everyone knows who you need to talk to and how to talk with them. Smaller congregations don't have to be "hung up" doing things by the book. They can be more flexible in their approaches to communication and decision making. (We will talk about the differences in the other average scores on the process scale in the following sections.)

With regard to strategy, we get a similar pattern:

STRATEGY

Planned   Spontaneous

_____

Corporate   Pastoral   Program   Family

Here again we see the Family Church at the loose end of the scale. Why plan when you already know what needs to be done? On this strategy scale the Family Church is in excess (as it was on the process scale).

We see the average small church not as thoughtful as larger churches when it comes to making sure that everybody understands which way the group is going. This may create excessive tension when the small church gets a leader who just went to a Ken Callahan "Twelve Keys to an Effective Church" seminar. The idea of serious planning just won't fit into this congregation's notion of how to approach figuring out what it wants to do next.

Though the scores are not different at a statistically significant level, it is interesting to note that the lay leadership in the smaller congregations perceives itself as more transformational than the other three groups. Yet they still are in excess at the managerial end of the scale!

Pastoral-Sized Congregations

The Pastoral-size Church has between 50 and 150 people on an average Sunday morning.[5] There may be two or three cells in this sized congregation. These primary groups are often extended-family units, but in some Pastoral Congregations the cells unite around a common interest such as music or a Sunday-school class or the women's organization. A leadership circle replaces the patriarch or matriarch and usually the pastor is at the center of this circle.

These congregations are often structured like a wheel rather than a pyramid. The hub is the minister with the spokes being the various cells that are in touch with and work with one another. In a congregation of this size the pastor is usually, quite literally, involved in everything. The pastor attends all the church meetings, goes to all public gatherings, and does most of the ministering. If people need to be called on, the pastor does it; if a couple need instruction on how to conduct and carry out a wedding and reception at the church, the pastor does it; if newcomers show up, the pastor calls on them. This is expected not only by the pastor but by the members and by the newcomers.

Those coming into a Pastoral-size Church will expect attention from the clergyperson; they will most likely bond first with him or her and later on with others in the church. This can cause a problem because the pastor cannot continue to give attention to those who are "in" but must work on bringing others in as well. This size church may have problems with assimilation and recruitment because the pastor is limited in the number of newcomers he or she can bring in at a time. Many pastors who have served this size church say that members tend to be casual, even uninterested, about newcomers, and that it is up to the pastor to get them interested.

Membership seems to be granted much more easily in the Pastoral Church than in the Family Church. But inclusion into the core circle may prove difficult and may take a significant amount of time.

Probably the most interesting (and most statistically significant) score for the Pastoral Church is on the authority scale. The highest (loosest or most dispersed) score of the four congregational sizes was 5.18 for the Pastoral-sized Church. According to the assumptions from which we are operating in this inventory, all four sizes of congregations (on the average) tend to manage this authority tension well. But it is interesting to note that the Pastoral Church is more dispersed than the others. This would mean that this congregation relies more on consultation than the other three, more people are involved in the decision making. This score may have been pushed higher because our sample of Pastoral Congregations included a large number of UUA congregations. But even without that factor, the figure is still high.

AUTHORITY

Concentrated   Dispersed

Program Family Corporate Pastoral

Clergy of Pastoral-size congregations are seen as more transformational than those of Program-size congregations (at a statistically significant level). We will address this issue more in the discussion of Program-sized congregations below.

For Pastoral-size congregations, process is more discretionary and strategy is less planned than for Corporate-size congregations. This probably has more to say about Corporate-size congregations than about Pastoral or Program-size congregations. Because of their size, corporate-sized congregations do not have the luxury of not paying attention to planning and communications. These things have to be worked out and planned ahead if the organization is to continue functioning at this size.

Program-Sized Congregations

The Program Church has between 150 and 350 people in church on an average Sunday. In this sized congregation, the pastor cannot attend to all of the organization or people; it is too large and there are too many. The congregation seems to pull itself into a more democratic organization than in the smaller churches. That is, members (and boards and committees) depend more on representatives to carry the various tasks of maintenance and ministry. More work is delegated by the pastor to laypeople and committees, and the governing board finds itself unable to "stay on top" of everything. It finds itself dependent on the work of others and the reporting of others.

In the Program Church the pastor spends less time in direct contact with members, especially with newcomers. To maintain the institution, the pastor must spend many more hours training, supervising, and co-ordinating the work of others. Sometimes congregations that are growing from the Pastoral to the Program model become annoyed with their pastor who seems less interested than previously in newcomers (and for that matter shut-ins and those who are hospitalized). It may not be that the pastor is less interested but rather that the pastor is overwhelmed by the pressing needs of coordination and management. Newcomers and shut-ins may make fewer immediate and visible demands than the staff, boards, buildings, funerals, and people coming in by appointment for counseling and weddings.

Congregational life in the Program Church may have less unity than in the Family or Pastoral church. There may be several centers of life or energy around which different members gather. In the Pastoral Church the members join the whole; they join the church. In the Program Church, members are more likely to join a part of the church—a church-school class, a choir, a couple's group, a study group, a group involved in outreach. Entry and assimilation occurs in a subgroup, rather than in the whole. The assimilators (those helping the newcomer with the entry into the congregation) are really helping people join smaller groups rather than helping them join the whole church.

Newcomers in the Program-size Church may go through several assimilation phases. They may first be welcomed into a short-term new members' or inquirers' class. After getting acquainted with a few people there, they may be officially welcomed into the church. The newcomers then find (if they have not already found) other "places to land." Sometimes this is a church-school class or other small group. If the newcomers have been recognized for their leadership potential in the new members' class or church-school class, they may be nominated for or invited to work on a church committee. Here another assimilation process is necessary, as the newcomers will not know and will not be known by most of the workers on the committee. One can see how easy it can be for the newcomer to get lost in a complex system. Unless the newcomer feels motivated to want to be an insider, she or he may easily stray from further participation.

To our surprise, from CSI data we found that pastoral leadership was significantly less transformational for the clergy of Program-sized congregations than for the other three categories. The most managerial clergy are those in Program-sized congregations followed by Pastoral-sized congregations and then Corporate-sized congregations. (The Family-sized congregations have the highest transformational scores, but this may be a fluke of our sample, which is highly biased toward Unitarian Universalists in this category. Note that UUA clergy are perceived to be more transformational than the other denominations in Pastoral- and Program-sized congregations.)

By and large the Program-sized congregations seem to be more tight than the other churches. Their authority is significantly more concentrated than both Corporate- and Pastoral-sized congregations. They have the lowest scores on the learning scale, meaning that they tend to maximize more and metamize less than the other congregations. They also have the lowest score on relatedness, meaning that they tend toward the "tight" end of that scale as well. (Yet, one cannot make a strong case for this because the differences between the sizes are not statistically significant on these two categories.)

Corporate-Size Congregations

In the largest churches, with more than 350 in attendance on Sunday morning, one finds an even more complex and diverse array of programs, ministries, classes, and committees. The senior pastor seems more distant from most members than in a smaller organization. The preaching, the building, the size of the organization, the credentials of the leaders, the reputation of the church—all instill respect and reverence and may cause the new person to be reticent about moving easily into the church.

Frequently in a church of this size ministers or leaders of departments function toward newcomers much like pastors in Pastoral-size congregations. The newcomer may join a department and get acquainted and assimilated there, much as he or she would in the Program Church. The senior pastor is known by relatively few people in the church; she or he functions as a symbol of unity and stability in an otherwise complex and seemingly fragmented organization.

As we have noted above Corporate-size congregations seem to have "tighter" organizations when it comes to strategy, authority, and process. This seems logical in that the larger the organization, the more necessary it is for people to plan and carefully communicate. Otherwise, they are going to be getting in each other's way. The authority scores are also more concentrated; larger organizations seem to find it more difficult to disperse authority proportionally throughout the system.

When it comes to learning, the Corporate Church is the most experimental of the four congregational sizes. (We noted above that the difference in scores cannot be said to be significantly different statistically.) From our experience with larger congregations, we do not find it surprising that they tend to be more venturesome than smaller churches. Often they hire more transformational staff. Indeed, when we control for the UUA influence on pastoral leadership scores, we find the scores of pastors in Corporate-sized congregations to be the highest of the three sizes that would have meaningful averages—Pastoral, Program, and Corporate.

Mean and Range Data for Each Dimension

Means for all scales:
Number of valid observations (listwise) = 515.00

Variable	Mean	Std Dev	Minimum	Maximum	Valid N
LAY LEADERSHIP	1.89	2.08	0	10	515
RELATEDNESS	4.01	2.06	0	10	515
LEARNING	4.57	3.00	0	10	515
AUTHORITY	4.63	2.38	0	10	515
PROCESS	5.96	2.11	0	10	515
PASTORAL LEADERSHIP	6.11	2.75	0	10	515
STRATEGY	6.71	1.92	1	10	515

Means for all scales by congregation size:

Summaries of   **STRATEGY**
By levels of   **CONGREGATIONAL SIZE**

Variable Value Label	Mean	Std Dev	Cases
For Entire Population	6.7146	1.9161	515
FAMILY SIZE	7.5294	1.5049	17
PASTORAL SIZE	6.8723	1.8970	188
PROGRAM SIZE	7.0490	1.8206	143
CORPORATE SIZE	6.1677	1.9409	167

Summaries of   **AUTHORITY**
By levels of   **CONGREGATIONAL SIZE**

Variable Value Label	Mean	Std Dev	Cases
For Entire Population	4.6272	2.3796	515
FAMILY SIZE	4.0000	2.2079	17
PASTORAL SIZE	5.1755	2.5069	188
PROGRAM SIZE	3.9860	2.2673	143
CORPORATE SIZ	4.6228	2.2025	167

Summaries of **PROCESS**
By levels of **CONGREGATIONAL SIZE**

Variable Value Label	Mean	Std Dev	Cases
For Entire Population	5.9612	2.1132	515
FAMILY SIZE	7.1765	1.6292	17
PASTORAL SIZE	6.0691	2.0320	188
PROGRAM SIZE	6.4336	2.0125	143
CORPORATE SIZE	5.3114	2.1618	167

Summaries of **PASTORAL LEADERSHIP**
By levels of **CONGREGATIONAL SIZE**

Variable Value Label	Mean	Std Dev	Cases
For Entire Population	6.1087	2.7545	515
FAMILY SIZE	6.7059	2.4178	17
PASTORAL SIZE	6.2872	2.6229	188
PROGRAM SIZE	5.3217	2.8939	143
CORPORATE SIZE	6.5210	2.6905	167

Summaries of **RELATEDNESS**
By levels of **CONGREGATIONAL SIZE**

Variable Value Label	Mean	Std Dev	Cases
For Entire Population	4.0078	2.0556	515
FAMILY SIZE	4.4118	2.0018	17
PASTORAL SIZE	4.1862	2.0351	188
PROGRAM SIZE	4.0420	2.0345	143
CORPORATE SIZE	3.7365	2.0890	167

Summaries of   **LAY LEADERSHIP**
By levels of   **CONGREGATIONAL SIZE**

Variable Value Label	**Mean**	**Std Dev**	**Cases**
For Entire Population	1.8874	2.0836	515
FAMILY SIZE	2.5882	2.4254	17
PASTORAL SIZE	1.9840	2.1507	188
PROGRAM SIZE	1.8182	1.9560	143
CORPORATE SIZE	1.7665	2.0767	167

Summaries of   **LEARNING**
By levels of   **CONGREGATIONAL SIZE**

Variable Value Label	**Mean**	**Std Dev**	**Cases**
For Entire Population	4.5650	2.9995	515
FAMILY SIZE	4.7059	2.9104	17
PASTORAL SIZE	4.3936	3.1495	188
PROGRAM SIZE	4.2238	2.8344	143
CORPORATE SIZE	5.0359	2.9389	167

Introducing the CSI:
A Suggested Meeting Design

Administering the Inventory

We suggest distributing the Congregational Systems Inventory (CSI) to participants in advance of the meeting where the results are to be explored.

Some additional reminders you might make when the packets are distributed:

— Ask participants to focus on the congregation as it is now.
— Ask them to make a choice for every item. (See "Trouble-Shooting Guide" in chapter V.)
— Invite participants to put their names on the inventory.

Before the meeting collect the completed and scored inventories so you can create a composite profile (see chapter V) that can be distributed to each participant at the meeting (and/or transferred to other audio-visual aids for presentation). Collecting the inventories ahead of time will also allow you to scan participant responses to ensure that choices were made for each item and that scoring procedures were followed.

If you cannot administer the inventory in advance of the meeting, you can create a composite profile as you present each of the seven scales by taking a show-of-hands consensus and registering the scores on a board, flip chart, or overhead projector. If participants complete and score the inventory in a meeting setting, allow twenty to twenty-five minutes for this in your schedule.

Presenting the Theory

Many people have told us how helpful the basic concepts in this material have been in their understanding of their congregations. As you present this material to your leaders, you might include these positive or useful points:

— your purpose for introducing and using this material
— the tyranny of successful habits
— the congregation as a system
— our tendency to see only part of the congregation's system
— the loose-tight paradox and the value of internal variety
— the value of tension between order and freedom
— the results of a loss of tension

In our initial presentations, we often draw examples from noncongregational settings. For example, we discuss basic style differences between spouses which, when kept in tension, produce more creative results.

Defining the Dimensions and Reflecting on Composite Scores for Each Scale

In your analysis meeting, you might invite participants to discuss each of the seven scales one at a time, stopping to examine and discuss the composite profile for each scale. We try to help people approach the CSI with a nonjudgmental attitude, recognizing that there are no right answers. We also encourage people to tell what they were thinking about when they filled out the inventory.

Our experience has been that people are helped by hearing concrete examples of potential excesses and of healthy tensions in congregational life. Refer to the examples in chapter IV.

As you move through each scale, offer your observations about the range and cluster of scores that point to indications of either excess or healthy tension. Invite discussion about the validity of the profile. Does it describe this congregation? What doesn't fit? You may also want to guide discussions about particular patterns of scores or individual responses to the inventory. (See "Trouble-Shooting Guide" in chapter V.)

Discussions generated by each of the seven scales may be as useful as the inventory results themselves. Because the CSI provides both a language to talk holistically about the congregation and composite data, people may be feel free to discuss issues and share observations that might otherwise be withheld.

Exploring the Overall Implications

Having looked at each of the seven scales individually, invite observations about the overall profile. What implications can be drawn from the relationship among the scales? This may be the first time that people have seen the church from this kind of vantage point, and they may be able to share new insights or piece together what had previously been only fragmentary impressions. We usually capture these observations and implications on newsprint to use later in a change process.

Chapters VI through XII defined numerous strategies for moving a congregation out of excess and toward healthy tension. You might share some of the ideas from this material at this introductory meeting or later as you help the leadership of the congregation develop an approach to change. People are naturally curious about what to do once they've identified evident excesses.

We often combine the results of the CSI with other theories and approaches to assessment including Arlin Rothauge's *Sizing Up Your Congregation*[1] and Martin Saarinen's *The Life Cycle of a Congregation*.[2] Combining these assessment approaches with good current information about the congregation and its environment can collectively produce a picture of the congregation. The CSI is much like a snapshot. It attempts to capture reality that is dynamic and fully understood only in motion. Yet the snapshot can produce a common shared picture of the current situation and prepare staff and lay leaders to make informed decisions about shaping a new future.

Chapter 1

1. Loren Mead, *The Once and Future Church* (Washington, DC: The Alban Institute, 1991), 84.

2. See Peter Senge, *The Fifth Discipline: The Art and Practice of the Learning Organization* (New York: Doubleday, 1990).

Chapter 2

1. Perhaps it is more than a need. Perhaps there is a connecting force or power that makes it impossible for human beings *in a relationship* to act without in some way affecting the other or others in the relationship.

2. Edwin Friedman, *From Generation to Generation* (New York: Guilford Press, 1985).

3. Ken Mitchell, *Multiple Staff Ministries* (Philadelphia: Westminster Press, 1988).

4. Merle A. Fossum and Marilyn J. Mason, *Facing Shame: Families in Recovery* (New York: W. W. Norton, 1986).

5. Demonstrations or riots are informal rituals if they are spontaneous, if the leadership emerges at the time of the event, and if no permit was secured from city hall for the demonstration. How are riots and demonstrations ritualistic? The activities in which the people are engaged do not directly affect the changes sought. Rather, they point to larger, more complex, meanings than those experienced in the event itself. (Dousing civil rights protesters with a fire hose or firing on students at Kent State—a police riot—or beating up patrons at a homosexual bar

or breaking windows and turning over cars after a ball game are ways of enacting meanings beyond the activities themselves. Setting fire to a car probably has nothing to do with cars in general, this particular car, or its owner.)

Chapter 4

1. Richard Pascale, *Managing on the Edge* (New York: Simon & Schuster, 1990).

Chapter 5

1. These categories and sizes (average Sunday morning attendance) are based on Arlin Rothauge, *Sizing Up a Congregation for New Member Ministry* (New York: Episcopal Church Center, n.d.). Family-sized, fewer than 50; Pastoral-sized, 50-150; Program-sized, 150-350; Corporate-sized more than 350.

2. For those familiar with the conflict levels described in Speed Leas, *Moving Your Church through Conflict* (Washington, DC: The Alban Institute, 1984), we do not recommend using this material in a conflict of level III or higher.

Chapter 6

1. See chapter 9, "Strategies to Move from Excess at the Mandatory End of the Scale," for an example of how to address the question of changing norms in a congregation.

Chapter 7

1. See chapter 12 for other ideas about creativity training.
2. See page 113 for a description of the way one group got acquainted with the life of teenagers in their community.

Chapter 11

1. See Lionel E. Deimel, "Construction Update Bulletin Board." *Congregations* (January-February 1993): 12. This article on bulletin boards is an example of a task that might be done alone.

Chapter 12

1. See George Prince, *The Practice of Creativity* (New York: Macmillan, Collier, 1970).

2. Kennon Callahan, *Twelve Keys to an Effective Church* (San Francisco: Harper & Row, 1983).

Chapter 13

1. Arlin Rothauge, *Sizing Up a Congregation for New Member Ministry* (n.d.), available from The Episcopal Church Center, 815 Second Ave., New York, NY 10017; $3.00 each plus $2.00 shipping and handling.

2. Roy Oswald and Speed Leas, *The Inviting Church* (Washington, DC: The Alban Institute, 1987).

3. Carl Dudley, *Making the Small Church Effective* (Nashville: Abingdon, 1978), 32.

4. Actually a significant difference could not be shown between the Family-sized congregations and the Pastoral- and Program-sized, because the sample (seventeen churches) is too small to show a statistically significant difference. There is a significant difference between the Family- and Corporate-sized congregations.

5. Don't take these numbers too literally. Some congregations have the numbers to exhibit the characteristics of a Pastoral Church, but act like a Family Church. This is sometimes a problem in growing churches in which they have trouble stretching to new ways of functioning under the altered demands of the larger system. Shrinking congregations also find themselves organized as a Program Church and attempt to function as such, but have lost so many people that the structure for the large institution no longer fits their diminished proportions.

Appendix

1. Arlin Rothauge, *Sizing Up a Congregation for New Member Ministry* (New York: Episcopal Church Center, n.d.).

2. Martin Saarinen, *The Life Cycle of a Congregation* (Washington, DC: The Alban Institute, 1986).

BIBLIOGRAPHY

Books Related to Organization Development Theory

Blake, Robert R., and Mouton, Jane Srygley. *Solving Costly Organizational Conflicts*. San Francisco: Jossey-Bass, 1984.

Levinson, Harry. *Organizational Diagnosis*. Cambridge, MA: Harvard University Press, 1972.

Schein, Edgar H. *Organizational Psychology*. Englewood Cliffs, NJ: Prentice-Hall, 1980.

Varney, Glenn H. *Organization Development for Managers*. Reading, MA: Addison-Wesley, 1977.

Weisbord, Marvin R. *Productive Workplaces: Organizing and Managing for Dignity, Meaning, and Community*. San Francisco: Jossey-Bass, 1987.

Books Related to Systems Theory

Anderson, Herbert. *The Family and Pastoral Care*. Philadelphia: Fortress Press, 1984.

Bernstein, Paula. *Family Ties, Corporate Bonds: How We Act Out Family Roles in the Office*. Garden City, NY: Doubleday, 1985.

Fossum, Merle A., and Mason, Marilyn. *Facing Shame: Families in Recovery.* New York: W. W. Norton, 1986.

Friedman, Edwin H. *Generation to Generation: Family Process in Church and Synagogue.* New York: Guilford Press, 1985.

Goldenberg, Irene, and Goldenberg Herbert. *Family Therapy: An Overview.* Monterey, CA: Brooks/Cole, 1991.

Kerr, Michael E., and Bowen, Murray. *Family Evaluation: The Role of the Family as an Emotional Unit That Governs Individual Behavior and Development.* New York: W. W. Norton, 1988.

Mitchell, Kenneth R. *Multiple Staff Ministries.* Philadelphia: Westminster Press, 1988.

Pascale, Richard Tanner. *The Art of Japanese Management: Applications for American Executives.* New York: Simon & Schuster, 1981.

Pascale, Richard Tanner. *Managing on the Edge: How the Smartest Companies Use Conflict to Stay Ahead.* New York: Simon & Schuster, 1990.

Senge, Peter M. *The Fifth Discipline: The Art and Practice of the Learning Organization.* Garden City, NY: Doubleday, 1990.

The CSI Participant Packet
ORDER FORM

The CSI is a survey designed to sample the perspectives of church staff, governing board, and key lay leaders. It enables you to assess where your congregation falls in a continuum between two behavioral extremes for each of the key areas. Sold in packages of 10 each 32-page CSI covers all seven areas and takes approximately 20 minutes to complete.

CSI AL147a $29.95 (package of 10)

CUSTOMER & SHIPPING INFORMATION

Circle one:
Rev. Rabbi Fr. Sr. Dr. Mr. Mrs. Ms.

_____

Address: _____

City: _____ State: ____ Zip + 4: _____
Daytimer telephone # ( ) _____
Denomination: _____

PAYMENT INFORMATION

☐ Payment enclosed   ☐ Bill me

Check # _____
or
Card # _____
(Visa/MasterCard only)

_____
Expiration date

_____
Signature on card

No. of packages:

_____

x $29.95

=   _____

-       _____
Member Discount
(see Alban catalog
or call)

+   _____
Shipping and Handling
($4.25 for first packet;
add $1.00 for each
additional packet)

=   _____
TOTAL
(U.S. funds only)

BY MAIL, send order to The Alban Institute, Suite 433 North, 4550 Montgomery Ave., Bethesda, MD 20814-3341.
BY PHONE, call 1-800-486-1318 or 301-718-4407 between 9 a.m. and 5 p.m. EST.
BY FAX, dial 301-718-1966.
Please have your credit card information ready (MasterCard or Visa only).